Brooklyn

People and Places, Past and Present

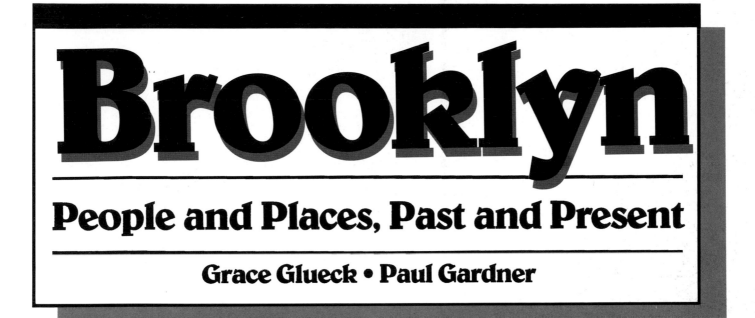

Brooklyn

People and Places, Past and Present

Grace Glueck • Paul Gardner

Harry N. Abrams, Inc., Publishers

To the memory of our parents

EDITOR:
MARK GREENBERG

ART DIRECTOR:
RAY HOOPER

DESIGNERS:
JANET VICARIO AND GREENFIELD & ASSOCIATES

PHOTO EDITOR:
UTA HOFFMANN

Library of Congress Cataloging-in-Publication Data

Glueck, Grace.
Brooklyn : people and places, past and present / Grace Glueck and Paul Gardner.
p.   cm.
Includes bibliographical references and index.
ISBN 0–8109–3118–4 (cloth)
Abradale ISBN 0–8109–8158–0
ISBN 0–8109–9178–0 (pbk)
1. Brooklyn (New York, N.Y.)—History—Pictorial works.
2. Brooklyn (New York, N.Y.)—Description—Views.   3. New York
(N.Y.)—History—Pictorial works.   4. New York (N.Y.)—Description—
Views.   I. Gardner, Paul, 1936– .   II. Title.
F129.B7G58   1991
974.7'23—dc20   91—10932

The lines from "Atlantis" are reprinted from *The Bridge, A Poem by Hart Crane*,
by permission of Liveright Publishing Corporation.
Copyright © 1933, 1958, 1970 by Liveright Publishing Corporation.

Epigraph from *A Tree Grows in Brooklyn* by Betty Smith: Reprinted by permission of HarperCollins Publishers.

Frontispiece
Brooklyn Dodgers manager "Lippy" Leo Durocher has a word with umpire
George Magerkurth during a 1939 game against the Boston Bees. *UPI/Bettman*

Page 6
The *Brooklyn Daily Eagle* plant and carriers. *The Brooklyn Public Library, Eagle Collection.*

Printed and bound in China
10 9 8 7 6 5 4 3 2 1

Harry N. Abrams, Inc.
100 Fifth Avenue
New York, N.Y. 10011
www.abramsbooks.com

Abrams is a subsidiary of

LA MARTINIÈRE
GROUPE

Contents

ACKNOWLEDGMENTS

▬

For their guidance and support, the authors wish to thank Caroline Blackman, Ruth Block, Michele and Sydney M. Cone, III, Seth S. Faison, Ruth Farbman, Dorothy Ferenbaugh, Phyllis and Wilbur Levin, John L. Livingston, Cynthia and Malcolm Mackay, The Rev. Donald W. McKinney, Audrey Madden, Barbara Millstein, Newell Mitchell, Steven Packard, Otis Pratt Pearsall, and John Willenbecher.

At Harry N. Abrams, Inc., we would like to thank our editor, Mark Greenberg, for his close attention to the details of this book; our photo researcher, Uta Hoffmann, for her perseverance in finding visual material; our designers, Ray Hooper, Janet Vicario, and Murray Greenfield and Caroline Bowyer, for their fine design; and our editor-in-chief, Paul Gottlieb, for his clear understanding and insight.

Grace Glueck   Paul Gardner

Introction

THE SUN ALWAYS SHINES ON BROOKLYN

There's no time to linger, ladies and gentlemen, find your seats in the van or we won't get to see the grave of Mae West or the haunted house of the Adams chewing gum family." A voluble tour guide is once again taking a mini-busload of passengers on a tour of Brooklyn, the legendary borough that used to be called "the forty-ninth state,"—and that now may be the fifty-first—that symbolizes those very American qualities of ambition, brashness, wiseguy humor, street smarts, and underneath the toughness, a soft touch. Everybody comes from Brooklyn, even those who don't. One out of every seven Americans was either born here, lived here once, had relatives here, or got here by taking the wrong subway. Say the word "Brooklyn" and the images flood the mind: Coney Island, the Dodgers, the Bridge, and the tree immortalized by Betty Smith.

Seated in the van, eager to revel in facts and folklore about "the fourth largest city in America," are two eminent researchers from Manhattan, digging at their roots; a show-me bishopess from Liverpool; a married couple from Castro Valley, California, who remember the beer gardens of Bushwick; and a scalp specialist from Long Island, scouting for real estate.

Motorcades of big tour buses now rumble through "the borough of churches and cemeteries," but our guide, whose earliest memories of anything anywhere are of Brooklyn, was one of the first to start junkets to restored brownstones, Tiffany-windowed mansions, banks that resemble cathedrals, and exotic delis where you can nibble on sinus-clearing succulents. "I couldn't live anywhere else," he says as the van passes Prospect Park. Pointing to a striking limestone residence, he adds, "Shirley MacLaine bought it in the 70s when she had a boyfriend nearby. Sure, it was a good investment." He presses the accelerator. "But, come along, let's visit Clinton Hill where Marianne Moore, one of our most famous poets, lived for almost thirty years. You'll see the last surviving double row of chestnut trees in the United States." Passing 250 Cumberland Street, he pulls up alongside Fort Greene Park, where, in the hol-

The Cyclone, Coney Island.
Photograph © David Lee

9

The Prison Ship Martyrs Monument in Fort Greene Park, built in 1908, recalls the 11,500 American patriots who died in the eleven British prison ships anchored in Wallabout Bay, 1776–83.
Photograph © David Lee

low of the hill, is a vast crypt for Americans who died as captives on British ships during the Revolutionary War. He indicates a pyramid of steps, once rolling farmland, now a memorial grave. "The comfort station atop the hill is, I believe, the only one of its kind designed by Stanford White."

Next, he shepherds his flock into the Lafayette Avenue Presbyterian Church in Fort Greene, where the stained-glass windows and glass chapel adornments are by Louis Tiffany. "Manhattan didn't cherish its Tiffany. But some of the finest examples of Tiffany glass are in Brooklyn," he observes with pride. A request: the bishopess from Liverpool wants to go back for snapshots to Grand Army Plaza whose Arch of Triumph reminds her of Paris. No one objects. The itinerary can be rearranged on a whim. Later, the van sweeps along Shore Parkway. On one side the Narrows—leading to the Atlantic Ocean—caress the coastline, and the elongated silhouette of the Verrazano Bridge looms in the distance. On the other side, the small bungalows of Bay Ridge, once a Scandinavian area, give way to waterfront estates built years ago by shipping tycoons and now rediscovered by new financial wizards.

"This is Brooklyn, too?" asks Liverpool.

"Most people don't know that Brooklyn has its fancy side," answers the guide. "Brooklyn has a peculiar effect on people. If you've never been here, you want to see it. If you've lived here once, you want to come back to refresh your memories."

He momentarily idles the motor in front of a brick house with freshly mown grass and lilac trees in bloom. "Two months ago a retired executive from Los Angeles wanted to see this house that he'd lived in until he was fourteen. That's when the Depression hit his family and they moved west. He asked the woman who lives here if he could go in and look around. As he wandered from room to room, she made coffee and brought out some rolls. 'Nothing's changed,' he said. Then he broke down and wept."

BURIED LEGENDS, LIVING LEGENDS.

The names associated one way or another with Brooklyn—Lillian Russell and George Gershwin, Margaret Sanger and Arthur Miller—jog the mind as the scenery flies by, from old Dutch farmhouses to soot-covered factory walls. The passing show that is Brooklyn, where a wilderness was cleared and cables were strung like jeweled necklaces from tower to tower first to connect disparate cities, then to separate them, remains an urgent spectacle in constant evolution.

"'*There goes the neighborhood*,' harrumphed the first Indian who saw the first boat sail into view," quips the guide. "The story of

Brooklyn has always been one of change. The Indians were overrun by the Dutch who were overrun by the English who, in turn, saw the Irish, the Germans, the Italians flooding in."

Brooklyn, in fact, has always been an accommodating melting pot of contrasting customs and cultures. It still is, with recent arrivals from Russia, Puerto Rico, Haiti, Syria, and Manhattan's Upper West Side. Perhaps symbolic of the mix is Nathan's Famous—the hotdog stand in Coney Island that all campaigning politicians feel compelled to visit. The tour stops there, too.

Leaning against a counter, the six passengers greedily gulp down juicy franks, emblazoned with squiggly ribbons of mustard. A salty breeze adds to the heady aroma.

"I see it, I taste it—Brooklyn!" exclaims an eminent researcher.

But there's so much to know about this amazingly complex borough.

Where does one begin?

Prospect Park entrance at Grand Army Plaza with the Stranahan statue seen from the rear. *New-York Historical Society*

The Making of Breukelen

FIRST, OF COURSE, THERE WERE THE INDIANS.

A branch of the Algonquin tribe known as the Canarsees had as their turf the western part of Long Island. Natty in deerskins and very "civil," the Canarsees greeted Henry Hudson when his ship, the *Half Moon*, dropped anchor in September 1609, in Gravesend Bay before going on to explore the river. They brought green tobacco and exchanged it for knives and beads. Some of Hudson's crew—half Dutch, half English—went ashore and described what later became Coney Island as "pleasant with Grasse and Flowers, and goodly trees as ever to be seen and very sweet smells came from them." It was Brooklyn's first recorded accolade.

The Indians didn't have Brooklyn—which they called Meryckawick, or "the sandy place,"—to themselves much after Hudson's visit. By the early 1620s, the Dutch West India Company, chartered by the government of Holland, had established the Colony of New Netherland, sprawling along the Hudson from New Amsterdam (Manhattan) to Fort Orange (Albany). In a famous transaction of 1626, Peter Minuit, director of the company, bought Manhattan from the Canarsees for $24 worth of goods. And soon the traders and farmers made their way across the river, where the flat, marshy plains reminded them of Holland, and where the soil could be tilled more easily than that of rock-bound New Amsterdam. In fact, the Dutch West India Company, eager to establish settlements, plugged Brooklyn in advertisements back home as having "the best clymate in the whole world," with "marvelous plenty in all kinds of food," and where "furrs of all sorts may bee had of the natives very reasonable."

The Indians were shrewder in disposing of Brooklyn than Manhattan. Waging a losing battle against the invasion of their land, they sold it bit by bit in separate deals—the total amounting to more than 200 times Manhattan's price. In some cases, they retained the rights to live or hunt. The first sales to Dutch settlers in

George Hayward (after Cornelia T. Meeker). The Old Bushwick Church, L.I. Built in 1711. Lithograph, 1864. Emmet Collection, Miriam and Ira D. Wallach Division of Art, Prints and Photographs. The New York Public Library, Astor, Lenox and Tilden Foundations

1636 were in the southeastern shore area now known as Flatlands.
Long before the end of the century, Brooklyn was firmly in European hands, and most of the Indians had headed west.

Early Brooklyn life grew up around a district that came to be known as The Ferry. It was named for the crude little public boat that—beginning in 1642—plied the East River from the foot of what's now Fulton Street to Peck Slip on the Manhattan side. To shelter storm-bound travelers, a tavern was built on the Brooklyn side, and it was quickly surrounded by a thriving little community.

LIBERATED LADY

The Dutch called the place "Breukelen,"—maybe meaning "broken valley," maybe "land of brooks and marshes"—after an ancient town in Holland. The houses clustered about a mile away from The Ferry, not far from what was later to be the site of Borough Hall. Other towns developed at the same time: Nieuw Amersfoort (Flatlands), Midwout (Flatbush), Nieuw Utrecht, Boswijck (Bushwick), and Gravesend. All were Dutch strongholds except Gravesend, which was founded by the redoubtable Lady Deborah Moody, Brooklyn's first liberated woman.

Lady Deborah—a strong-willed widow who sought in America the religious and civil liberties she felt were lacking in her native England—had immigrated to the Massachusetts Bay Colony in 1639 with her son, Sir Henry Moody. Her reformist beliefs soon collided with those of the rigid Puritan church. After being involved in other religious clashes in seaboard settlements, this grand dame wound up in the Coney Island area. From New Amsterdam's governor, she got a land patent—the first ever given to a woman—which she shared with her son and some forty fellow-dissenters. Unique in the New World, it guaranteed the settlers the right to worship as they pleased, and it also allowed them a town-meeting form of government.

Lady Deborah then laid out, in cartwheel fashion, the stockaded town she called Gravesend, after the Moody family's place of origin in Kent, England (where, curiously enough, the American Indian princess Pocahontas had earlier been buried). She established a school, built a church, and set up the town government. In her spare time, she read Latin, tended a large personal library, and kept up with nonconformist movements. She died in 1659, and a graveyard with her stone is still located on Gravesend Neck Road between Sicklen Street and MacDonald Avenue.

TERRITORIAL SEESAW

A few years later, the entire New Netherland colony shifted abruptly from Dutch to British rule: King Charles II of England, ignoring Dutch claims to New Netherland, granted to his brother the duke of York the whole area from the Connecticut to the Delaware rivers. In 1664 a British fleet was sent to enforce his claim, and the province was bloodlessly surrendered.

New Amsterdam became New York, Fort Orange was redubbed Albany. But for the next decade the territory seesawed between the English and the Dutch. In 1674, the English won out, and they ruled until their banishment by the American Revolution a century later. By 1683 they had established the present boundaries of Kings County—i.e., Brooklyn—comprising the original six towns.

The placid little settlements, mostly occupied with farming, grew slowly. Virtually everyone, including black slaves and the remaining Indians, spoke Dutch, at least until the Revolutionary War. The average Dutch farm occupied twenty acres, and the lifestyle, not too different from that of Holland, was centered on the home, usually a one-story gabled affair built of wood or stone, lighted by narrow windows and protected by strong palisades against wild beasts and Indian prowlers.

Inside, the houses were dominated by huge fireplaces—big enough to accommodate the whole family in cold weather—with capacious chimneys, in which meat was hung for roasting or smoke-curing. In the parlor or living room, which also served as a guest room, a big four-poster bed with its down quilts, accompanying furniture and hangings, served as evidence of the family's status.

The Hicks-Platt residence at 17 Gravesend Neck Road, which, in the 1890s, was publicized as Lady Moody's house by real-estate developer William E. Platt. *Photograph © David Lee*

The floors were carpeted with white sand, brought from nearby beaches. Each house also had a high front stoop—a remnant of the Hollandish concern for floods—where on good days families gathered with their friends.

And hospitality ran high. After visiting Breukelen a Dutchman traveling with a friend wrote appreciatively of a generous host. Warming themselves before a roaring oak-and-hickory fire, the travelers ate roasted Gowanus oysters—"fully as good as those of England"—a roasted haunch of venison bought from the Indians, wild turkey and wild goose, and sampled watermelon "as large as pumpkins." They slept soundly that night in a Kermis—or trundle bed—in a corner of the hearth "alongside of a good fire."

Aside from some domestic crops, the Dutch farmers raised and exported tobacco, some of the best of it coming from a plantation around the Wallabout. They also grew cotton, but mainly for household use. A key import was slaves, who did much of the farm labor. However, the outlook of the Dutch settlers was simple and democratic. Everyone mingled freely without regard to money or station. The notion of aristocracy was presumably brought into the colony

The Defeat of the American Army and the Occupation of New York City by British Forces under General Sir William Howe, September 1776. *Colored engraving. Granger Collection, New York*

by the English, who refused to abandon their caste-conscious life at home.

Unlike the English, the Dutch were not politically active. The average Dutch settler was a stubborn individualist, intent only on planting his farm and building his house. Bruekelen was, however, the first of the towns to seek the privilege of electing its own officers, thereby initiating a limited form of self-government.

Though it was the most populous of the towns, Breukelen—or Brooklyn, as it had become under the English—was still no more than an agricultural village by the time of the Revolution. While the center of the village was a mile from the ferry on the Jamaica Road, some fifty houses stood in the Ferry district, and a few dotted the groves of cedars that crowned nearby Brooklyn Heights. Farmhouses were scattered along the shore of the river to Gowanus, and on the Wallabout shore to Bushwick. From the river to Fulton and Joralemon streets lay orchards, pastures, and market gardens. Little did the stolid farmers dream that this idyllic scene would soon become a battlescape.

BATTLE CRY

Though the Dutch of Kings County knew that the continuing oppressions of the British government must lead to an uprising, they were not eager for a showdown. Personal inconvenience and monetary loss were reasons to avoid war. Their apathy, in fact, encouraged the English loyalists and disheartened supporters of the American side. In late August 1776, the county became the setting for the first major invasion of the Revolutionary War—the Battle of Brooklyn.

Encamped on Staten Island in July, the British forces waited a month to make their move, a march on to a point between what is now Fort Hamilton Parkway and 22nd Avenue, on the southwest coast of Brooklyn. After heavy fighting, the sparse American troops were outmaneuvered by the British. From his command post on Brooklyn Heights, General George Washington took prompt measures to avert more bloodshed. He devised a brilliantly staged retreat under cover of darkness, and with the help of a dense fog, the American force was evacuated to Manhattan. The last to leave was Washington himself.

But after New York also fell, Brooklyn's Wallabout Bay became a horror scene. The British began to confine captured American seamen in rotting hulks that served as prison ships. Over a six-year period, an estimated 12,000 victims died in the teeming wrecks, starved, beaten and bayoneted, and ravaged by disease. Every day, bodies were ferried to the shore and buried in sand pits dug by surviving prisoners under the watchful eyes of guards. The bones

Prison ship. *Engraving*

quickly washed out of the shallow graves and could be seen along the beaches for years.

In 1855, however, influential citizens of Brooklyn resolved to bury the bones and raise a suitable monument. A site in Fort Greene Park was chosen, but not until nearly twenty years later did the bones reach their final resting place. A superstructure memorializing the prisoners, known as the Prison Ship Martyrs Monument, was designed by the firm of McKim, Mead & White in 1908. It's the world's tallest Doric column.

Aside from the Wallabout death ships, the seven years of British occupation scarred the country in other ways. In the town of Brooklyn itself, British and Hessian troops plundered houses, seized crops and animals, destroyed the fences that bounded farms, and felled entire woods for fuel. Soldiers were billeted on the townspeople, who were also assessed for a huge fort built by the British at Pierrepont and Henry streets, and churches were used for barracks, storehouses, prisons, and hospitals. Town records were removed. Civic privileges and functions were suspended.

FRESH FIELDS

At the Revolution's close, citizens of Brooklyn had to make order out of chaos. They were faced with the tasks of reestablishing farm

boundaries, recultivating land, and restoring their personal affairs. There was also the need to reorganize the town, whose political life had died during the military occupation. In April 1784 the first town meeting in eight years was held. But, as the Revolution faded from memory, so did enmities between British and Colonial supporters, and life began to resume a normal course.

By 1800, according to General Jeremiah Johnson, mayor of Brooklyn for three terms after the War of 1812, the population of Kings County amounted to 4,495, including 930 "free white males of ten and upwards," 1,449 free white females, and 1,432 slaves. The white population was mostly Dutch, Johnson wrote, with some "attached to their old prejudices; but within a few years past, liberality and a taste for the fine arts have made considerable progress." And he added, "The slaves are treated well, but the opinion relative to their freedom is yet too much influenced by pecuniary motives."

At this point, Brooklyn was still a stronghold of pastoral beauty, and it continued that way for the first third of the nineteenth century. Houses, taverns, stables, and shanties formed a nucleus of business activity at the site of the Old Ferry. And from the ferry slip, an ancient country road—the "king's highway" of the Colonial period —became the great highway of travel to Long Island.

H. Bartlett and G. K. Richardson. The Ferry at Brooklyn, New York. *Steel engraving, London, 1838. American Antiquarian Society, Worcester, Massachusetts*

The Ferry Boat at Brooklyn. *Collection of the Municipal Archives of the City of New York, W.P.A. Federal Writers' Project*

Stock certificate of the Brooklyn Ferry Company of New York, issued 1898. *New-York Historical Society*

The Ferry Crossing

The growth of any community depends on how easily you can move to and fro. Economics, politics, and ethnicity played strong roles in shaping the borough that leisurely rolled over low hills and marshy fields, but none was perhaps initially as important as transportation. Settlers not only had to figure out how to get around Brooklyn, but how to shuttle back and forth across the East River to Manhattan—a question that mass transit hasn't entirely resolved today, with a subway system that is smelly, sweaty, and fairly spooky, depending on the hour and station.

A farmer named Cornelis Dircksen, who toiled on the Manhattan side, saw the commercial advantages to a ferry and started the first service in a flat-bottomed rowboat in 1642. The boat was moored near a tree. To rout farmer Dircksen from his plowing, you simply tooted a horn hanging from a tree branch. Eventually he built a saloon that doubled as a wayside inn for Brooklyn's earliest commuters. As the years passed, the boats got larger and safer, though their passage still depended on fickle winds and tides.

When Robert Fulton's steamboat began ferry service in 1814, Brooklyn was finally an easy commute to Manhattan. You could lean on a rail and inhale the ocean breeze or, on chilly days, warm yourself in a cabin beside a coal stove. Fulton had control of the steamboats, but there were also cheaper rival ferries that had teams of horses, walking on treadmills, turning the paddle wheels.

The trip took about fifteen minutes, except when the river was caked with ice. Then it could last more than an hour. Stagecoaches linked commuters from Gowanus to the ferry landing. By the time the Brooklyn Bridge opened, there were over a dozen ferryboats operating. But with the building of tunnels and other bridges—the Manhattan and the Williamsburg—service dwindled and finally stopped in 1940.

Today the ferries operate again, but they're high-speed boats, skimming the river from the old Fulton Street Landing in Brooklyn Heights and Bay Ridge to the Wall Street area. Passengers have the comfort of cushioned seats and can buy sweets, coffee, beer, and soda.

Eventually boats may stop at piers in Midtown Manhattan. Walt Whitman was prescient when he predicted in his poem "Crossing Brooklyn Ferry," in 1856, that they would endure and "... others will see the sun half an hour high ... will enjoy the sunset ... the pouring-in of the flood-tide, the falling back to the sea of the ebb-tide."

High-speed Catamaran TNT Express in New York harbor. *Hydrolines, Atlantic Heights, New Jersey*

OF HOMES AND CHURCHES

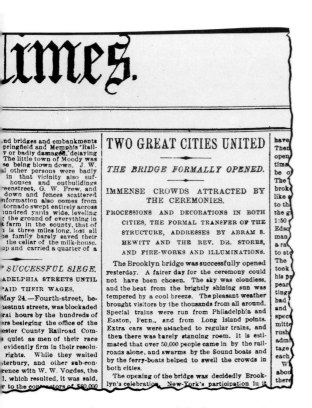

Announcement of the formal opening of
the Brooklyn Bridge, February 25,
1883. *The New York Times*

Preceding page
John Bornet. City of Brooklyn, Long
Island. *Lithograph, 1855. Eno Collection,
Miriam and Ira D. Wallach Division of
Art, Prints and Photographs. The New
York Public Library, Astor, Lenox and
Tilden Foundations*

Still, things were beginning to change in the county, which for nearly one hundred fifty years had existed as a sleepy backwater of the
bustling metropolis across the river. Though the War of 1812, triggered by British interference with American sea trade, again
brought the British to American soil, the lower part of New York
State—including Brooklyn and Long Island—avoided becoming a
major battlefront. After the war ended, Brooklyn—with a population of about four thousand in 1816—was incorporated as a village.
It was about a mile square, with shops, houses, and taverns lining
what is now Fulton Street. In rapid succession, it got a board of
health, a fire department, a fire insurance company, and its first real
bank. A large market was built, a municipal court was established,
and new streets and avenues began to march across farmlands.

By now, the village sported seven churches, seven distilleries,
eight rope factories, two tanneries, two tide-and-wind mills, an iron
foundry, and plants for the manufacture of chain cable, white lead,
glass, pharmaceuticals, floor cloth, cards, pocketbooks, combs,
sealskin, and dying equipment. Doing retail business were grocery
and dry-goods stores, printing establishments, and lumberyards.

By the mid-30s, Brooklyn had, in fact, become, as the social his-
torian Ralph Foster Weld has put it, "the city of homes and
churches, a lecture-going, church-going community, a pleasant
suburban place, quieter and more sedate than New York. The di-
sheveled, unkempt village of 1816 had undergone a metamorpho-
sis." And for some time, there had been pressure from Brooklyn's
leading citizens for its incorporation as a city. But the move was
hotly opposed by New York, whose officials feared a challenge to
the profitable water and ferry rights granted by England in 1686.
Manhattan real estate developers also worried that Brooklyn land
might prove more attractive than the large parcels they held above
14th Street. In fact, the counterproposal was made that Brooklyn be
incorporated into the City of New York. But in 1834, Brooklyn won
its battle with the legislature and was a city in its own right.

The event marked the end of the old village days and the beginning of urban life. The new city soon had a mayor, a board of alder-
men, and a city hall. It had a population of 30,000 by 1840, a district
of 12 square miles and 35 miles of paved and lighted streets. Brooklyn was also beginning to show signs of its industrial future: docks,
warehouses, and factories lined the shore of the East River.

Meanwhile, successive waves of immigration were transforming
Kings County from a domain of Dutch–English Protestant ways
and values to one of the nations's most cosmopolitan urban areas.
During the 1830s and 40s poor immigrants from southern Ireland

came in droves, many settling in South Brooklyn and bringing the county its first strong Roman Catholic presence. Between 1840 and 1860, over a million Germans arrived in the United States, a large proportion of them taking up residence in Brooklyn. Before the turn of the century came Poles and Slavs, then Scandinavians, then Italians, all forming a matchless labor pool for the city's developing industries.

First Naval Conflict Between the Iron-Clad Vessels *Merrimac* and *Monitor* in Hampton Roads, March 9, 1862. *New-York Historical Society*

Brooklyn's rapidly escalating growth brought about its absorption of Williamsburg and Bushwick. It was the fastest growing city in the country. When the Civil War broke out, this liberal northern metropolis naturally supported the Union, contributing soldiers to the cause and opening homes and hospitals to the sick and wounded. The industrial community of Greenpoint was the birthplace of the odd-looking ironclad vessel *Monitor*—dubbed "the Yankee cheese-box on a raft"—which in 1862 engaged the Confederate frigate *Merrimac* at Hampton Roads in the world's first battle between ironclad ships.

During and after the Civil War years, Brooklyn acquired roads and recreational areas: Prospect Park, 526 acres of rolling meadows, picturesque heights, and luxuriant greenery; Eastern and Ocean parkways; and the Concourse at Coney Island. The father of these amenities was James S. T. Stranahan, a business and civic leader who founded Brooklyn's park and boulevard system. He later became one of the chief promoters of the Brooklyn Bridge and pressed for Brooklyn's consolidation with New York.

BRIDAL BELLS

The idea of a bridge wedding Brooklyn with Manhattan had been broached as far back as the early 1800s, but it was rejected by old-guard Brooklynites who wished to keep the distance of the river. "Between New York and Brooklyn there is nothing in common, either in object, interest or feeling—nothing that even apparently tends to their connection, unless it be the water that flows between them," wrote General Jeremiah Johnson in the *Brooklyn Star* in 1834. But Brooklyn's exuberant expansion, her pressing need for a more permanent connection than the ferries with Manhattan and

John Augustus Roebling. *Engraving,*
1883. Granger Collection, New York

The Brooklyn Bridge.
Photograph © Ruth Block

indeed the vast continent of North America, made the bridge inevitable.

In 1865, John A. Roebling, an engineer who was just completing the Cincinnati–Covington Bridge over the Ohio River—at the time the world's longest span—prepared a set of plans and put them before some Brooklyn civic leaders. Two years later, a bill was passed by the state legislature to incorporate the New York Bridge Company for the purpose of "constructing and maintaining a bridge over the East River between the cities of New York and Brooklyn." A completion date of June 1870 was set. But it was not until 1883, after years of struggle and dissension, that the great bridge was completed. Ironically, this Brooklyn-inspired and chiefly Brooklyn-backed accomplishment was destined to bring to an end Brooklyn's life as a separate city.

The idea of consolidation of the two cities—mostly urged by New York—was broached by officials at various times in the ensu-

ing decades. Yet there was plenty of opposition, both in Brooklyn and New York. Many Brooklynites felt that to merge with New York was to submerge their own city, and their fears were enhanced by the corruption of New York City's government under the Tammany political machine. Only in 1890 was a commission created by the state to look into the feasibility of consolidation. Then it took six more years before enough votes were mustered in the legislature to make it happen. On New Year's Day, 1898, Brooklyn officially— to the regret of many of her citizens—became one of the five boroughs of the City of New York.

Brooklyn has had its ups and downs since then, but its vigorous spirit lives. Its development under the Dutch as a stronghold of religious freedom enabled it to welcome the most diverse personalities and ethnic groups, and the mix has given this beloved borough an identity—at home and abroad—that hasn't faded.

THE BROOKLYN BRIDGE

*Through the bound cable strands, the arching path
Upward, veering with light, the flight of
   strings,—
Taut miles of shuttling moonlight syncopate
The whispered rush, telepathy of wires.
Up the index of night, granite and steel—
Transparent meshes—fleckless and gleaming
   staves—
Sibylline voices flicker, waveringly stream
As though a god were issue of the strings . . .*

When the gifted American poet Hart Crane was finishing his epic, *The Bridge*, in the mid-20s, he wrote a friend about the freedom and life he experienced walking across "the most beautiful bridge in the world, the cables enclosing us and pulling us upward in such a dance—." Influenced by the French symbolists, and by Walt Whitman who grew up in Brooklyn, Crane likened the Brooklyn Bridge to a mystical and ecstatic love, uniting America's past to the present. The tortured young poet from Ohio was living at 110 Columbia Heights in the shadow of *that bridge*, and he was transfixed by the "symbol of our constructive future, our unique identity, in which is also included our scientific hopes and achievements of the future." Today, many bridges later, the Brooklyn Bridge—completed after fourteen years, in 1883—is still generally considered the most beautiful suspension bridge in the world.

John A. Roebling, an immigrant from Germany who had built the bridge at Niagara Falls, designed—daringly for that time—the world's longest and first steel suspension span with a perfect curve. A Currier & Ives lithograph, printed some years before the towering structure was completed, described it as "The Great East River Bridge." But to Brooklynites and, in no time flat, to the rest of the world, it was the Brooklyn Bridge—or simply, The Bridge. This startling web of steel, symbol of strength and courage, has been a backdrop for musical dramas, *Godspell*, for example, and plays like *Winterset*. Almost immediately it became the subject of a popular song, *Strolling on the Brooklyn Bridge*, and has since stimulated artists like the watercolorist John Marin and the abstractionist Joseph Stella. The novelist Henry Miller has extolled the bridge and so has the French architect Le Corbusier. A few years ago, a bimonthly English-language "fan" magazine was published in Holland called "The Brooklyn Bridge Bulletin."

When Norman Rosten, Brooklyn's poet laureate, walked across the bridge not so long ago with the British comedian Michael Palin, the Monty Python cut-up was awed. "It looks so solid, the cables, the supporting bars and suspenders, and those high stone towers, as solid as anything man could build, yet it seems as we stand here, weightless, as though it would float away if it weren't moored to the land." About a century earlier, another British performer, the celebrated Ellen Terry, on an American tour, walked across the bridge many times. She liked it coated with ice and snow, when it resembled "a gigantic trellis of dazzling white."

Blustery winter storms that froze the East River—ferryboat service stopped—helped

The Brooklyn Bridge by Night. *Photograph © Carollee Pelos*

convince political powers on both sides of the water that a bridge was needed. Public and private issues ultimately financed the spectacular enterprise. Under the famous "Boss" Tweed who then ruled New York, some stocks were fraudulently manipulated and numbers of investors were suddenly wiped out. But the construction gave jobs to hundreds of immigrants, twenty of whom lost their lives during the underwater digs.

An early casualty was the engineering genius himself, John Roebling, who died shortly after an accident during the building of the bridge. His son, Washington Roebling, quickly stepped in and supervised the foundations for the stone towers. But he was severely crippled by the "bends" from prolonged underwater exposure. Undaunted, Roebling then directed the fusion of aesthetics and mechanics with pen, paper, and telescope from an apartment on Columbia Heights (in the same building where Hart Crane later lived). Through it all his wife, Emily, made daily visits to the bridge, carrying his communiqués. Transcending tragedy and sacrifice, the bridge finally existed! "This was not the first work of engineering to be a work of art," summed up the architectural critic Lewis Mumford. "But it was the first product of the age of coal and iron to achieve this completeness of expression."

The Bridge became *the* sight to see, touch, and experience. Crowds thronged to it. One packed day, a week after the opening, someone tripped. There was a cry. Then hysterical screams: "The bridge is falling!" Twelve people were killed during a stampede to flee the bridge, and almost forty were injured. The rock-solid strength of the bridge was demonstrated the following year when the circus impresario P. T. Barnum marched his colossal headliner Jumbo and twenty other elephants across the masterwork that rivaled the Eiffel Tower in structural beauty.

The bridge continues to draw thousands of visitors, promenaders, and commuters who go back and forth by car or on foot. "Living in downtown Brooklyn I see it often, but it's still a cause for wonder," says politico Elizabeth Holtzman. "I frequently drive across, but what's most impressive is the half-hour walk, preferably on a clear summer day, because then you have an opportunity to look up *into* the bridge, to involve yourself in that amazing meshwork of cables."

The powerful arches of the bridge framed against the spires of Manhattan, the boats sailing below, the surrounding harbor opening to the Atlantic create a vivid scene that heightens the senses. The artist, wrote Hart Crane, "needs gigantic assimilative capacities, emotion—and the greatest of *all—vision*." And his extremely personal vision was ignited by the bridge, which became his synthesis of the world.

Schell and Hogan. A Promenade in Mid-Air: The Brooklyn Ascent to the Bridge Tower. *Lithograph. Museum of the City of New York*

Hart Crane, whose poetry of emotional force ended with his suicide in 1932 when he jumped from a steamer off the Florida coast. *Columbia University Libraries, Rare Book and Manuscript Library, New York*

Home, Sweet Brooklyn

There's a tree that grows in Brooklyn.
Some people call it the tree of Heaven.
No matter where its seeds fall, it makes a tree
which struggles to reach the sky. It grows in
boarded up lots and out of neglected rubbish heaps.
It grows up out of cellar gratings. It is the
only tree that grows out of cement. It grows lushly . . .
survives without sun, water, and seemingly without
earth. It would be considered beautiful except
that there are too many of it.

—Betty Smith

ire escape sitting time, recalls the novelist Betty Smith in her 1943 classic *A Tree Grows in Brooklyn*—a serene hour when the eleven-year-old heroine (who represents the author herself), puts a small rug on the fire escape of her tenement in the Williamsburg section and imagines that she is living in a tree. And, once out there, living in the tree, where no one could see her, the little girl is at peace: "she could look out through the leaves and see everything."

The ailanthus tree, curling and twisting upward in this urban setting of 1912, is lovelier than an entire forest, or, for that matter, a tree anywhere in the world. For those ragamuffins who didn't have the tree's enchantment in their backyard, then the refuge was the library, or the corner candy store. Through the years these sanctuaries remain, but best of all is the ailanthus—a symbol of courage and optimism, determined to grow higher and, perhaps, touch the sky.

The novelist, who was born Betty Wehner of German–Irish parents, acknowledged the poverty around her in the Greenpoint and Williamsburg neighborhoods, made clearly visible by the hock shops and junk dealers, but she managed also to see the beauty of a tree and the afternoon sun shining upon it on a summer day. Smith

Betty Smith, author of *A Tree Grows in Brooklyn, Culver Pictures*

The famous stoops of Brooklyn—in Greenpoint. *Photograph © Tony Velez*

An ailanthus—the tree that "grows in Brooklyn." *Photograph © David Lee*

left Williamsburg when she was in her teens and did not return to the borough until her novel was published. Brooklyn, she said, was her "lodestar" and she could never forget any of it, but, she added a trifle wistfully, it seemed more wonderful "when you're away from it."

Many of her generation felt the same. Barbara Stanwyck was orphaned by her poor Scottish–Irish parents at the age of four, and she summed up as "awful" her first fourteen years in Brooklyn. "In eleven years I lived in fourteen different homes," she once said. "My clearest memory is of the crowds, of spent old women bent over hot tubs and babies crying and men reeling drunk to their

homes. Half the time I slept on a mattress on the kitchen floor."
Her goals were to "eat, to survive and to have a good coat." Under
her real name of Ruby Stevens, she began to eat regularly, at least,
as a chorus girl who also rode an elephant in *The Ziegfeld Follies of
1922.* (Her melodic mezzo voice, refined in Hollywood, enabled
her to play brittle socialites and dangerous dames who turned life
into a wild crap shoot.) Stanwyck didn't revisit Brooklyn. Nothing
could drag her back to any neighborhood for a quick glimpse. Yet
the star of steely confidence whose independent spirit was forged
on some of the borough's mean streets said with terse candor, "I'm
a tough broad from Brooklyn." For countless others, such as the
novelist Bernard Malamud, author of *The Fixer*, who was raised in
Flatbush, there is the warm nostalgia for a countryside that he saw
expand into a series of neighborhoods without signs or boundaries.
Malamud remembers a sense of nature, of trees and fields. "My
feeling was that Brooklyn had the quality of a small town, where I
lived. There were unpaved roads and the Long Island Railroad had
its freight trains coming through an open cut, which added to the
country effect. I thought of Brooklyn as *a home town*."

Gradually, where there had once been dumps and marshes and
fields, pockets of thriving civilization emerged at the turn of the
century. The Pulitzer Prize–winning playwright Arthur Miller
(*Death of a Salesman*) reflects that Brooklyn was "a little different
than coming from elsewhere because it was a lot of villages, each
with a variety of people, working people and professionals, Italians,
Jews. You saw all sorts of people." Today the demographics of communities have changed and you see even more sorts of *all* sorts,
from the sculptor Judy Pfaff, who welds her discs, spheres, and
squiggles at a studio in Williamsburg, where she captures the color
and feeling of a neighborhood struggling to survive, to the Broadway producer Rocco Landesman, who mulls hit projects (*Big River*,
Into the Woods) and the health of that fabulous invalid, the American
theater, from his house in Brooklyn Heights, far from the noisy
madness of Broadway. Brooklyn, points out Norman Rosten, is a lot
of small towns without boundaries. "It is definitely a place, as well
as a *mystique*."

SWEET GLIMMERINGS RECAPTURED

Brooklyn Heights remains a neighborhood seemingly untouched
by the hurly-burly of life in the late twentieth century. Situated on a
bluff with a view of the river, it was where many shipping merchants (in the 1800s) built mansions that led down to the piers and
warehouses whose roofs were bedecked with flowers, trees, and
lawns. Gradually the brick and brownstone houses and clapboard

Bernard Malamud. *UPI/Bettmann*

35

Walt Whitman: The "Carpenter Portrait," which accompanied the first edition of *Leaves of Grass. Engraving, 1855. New-York Historical Society*

cottages, similar to the historic frame houses in Newport, Rhode Island, became duplexes and apartments. Many old aristocrats moved away, and The Heights became a cozy neighborhood for families, and artists, writers, and other "bohems." Today it's sought after by the young Wall Street crowd, which only has a short commute across the river. Of the famous hotels in The Heights, part of the St. George has been turned into luxury condos, the Bossert is owned by the Jehovah's Witnesses, and the Hotel Margaret was destroyed by fire during renovations in 1980. From a studio high in the Hotel Margaret, the artist Joseph Pennell produced etchings in the 1920s of the to-ings and fro-ings in the harbor. The scene, he believed, was more intriguing than anything he'd seen from the London Embankment.

Basically, The Heights—with more than 600 houses built before 1860—was a peaceful village until the 1950s when the Brooklyn–Queens Expressway separated it from the waterfront. Shortly thereafter, real estate developers arrived with bulldozers, nonchalantly crushing American history, including a small red brick house where Walt Whitman's *Leaves of Grass* was printed in 1855. And up went a row of urban ugliness—skyscrapers that became know as Cadman Plaza, which might look half decent anywhere else, but not in The Heights.

Still, if you're looking for the ambience of a genteel village, you can find it in Brooklyn Heights, though with prices escalating, the delightful mom-and-pop shops are rapidly being displaced by junk food emporiums and chain stores on its "main street," Montague, named after the English poet Lady Mary Wortley Montague, who was related to the Pierreponts. A woman of spirit, Lady Montagu is remembered for a remark uttered in 1778: "People wish their enemies dead—but I do not; I say give them the gout, give them the stone!"

A child said, what is the grass? —Walt Whitman

The name of the poet, carpenter, and editor Walt Whitman (1819–1892) pervades Brooklyn history, but there are no parks or plazas honoring him—though a library branch in Fort Greene does bear his name. A farmboy from Long Island, he moved to The Heights with his family and lived on Cranberry Street, behind the Plymouth Church. For some years he worked with his father as a carpenter, building small houses in Brooklyn. His forefathers were Quakers, but he leaned toward the "healthy this-worldliness" of his Dutch mother. On desolate stretches of Coney Island, he would cry out the words of Homer and Shakespeare to the pounding surf. His poetry, he sometimes said, was oceanic, recalling the waves, rising and falling, often sunny and then suddenly erupting into storm. In 1840 he plunged into causes: reform, free trade, restrictions of slavery. He scorned rank and privilege and preached on the rights of man. Whitman was convinced that America was the "custodian of the future of humanity." In his print shop, at Fulton and Cranberry, where there's now a subway exit, he set into type and published the first poems of his epic *Leaves of Grass*. Walt Whitman saw a symbol of democracy in the summer grass.

Before the Civil War, many streets in The Heights were named after the local gentry, such as Montague and Pierrepont. The coming of such streets as Orange, Pineapple, Cranberry, Poplar, and Willow is steeped in contradictory Brooklyn folklore. Everyone agrees that a Miss Middagh was the dowager who went around altering the signs, but everyone disagrees as to *why*. In one version, she felt that the streets should have botanical names. In another, she became peeved with some members of the aristocracy so she tore down signs bearing their names. A third version suggests that the landowners themselves didn't want their names on street signs and selected the names of fruits and trees. Miss Middagh was scandalized at the loss of the Middagh name. It would not, she fumed, be replaced by, let us say, Tangerine or Evergreen. She obstinately tore down her new sign and put back the old. Anyway, Middagh Street remains between Poplar and Cranberry.

The documentation for one house on The Heights has the stuff of a TV mini-series. At the turn of the century Herman Behr, a millionaire manufacturer of sand-and-garnet paper, had a vast fortress of a mansion built for him at 84 Pierrepont. Rounded bay windows, massive archways, and terra-cotta ornamentation made it a sumptuous sanctuary for the sherry sippers of society. Eventually the family dispersed, and after World War I it was enlarged and became the swank Palm Hotel. Still later the fickle fate of fortune turned the hotel into a gentlemen's house of pleasure. It was resurrected to respectability after being acquired by the Franciscan Brothers. And today? It's a desirable condominium, but try to find one available. Under its roof, the Behr mansion holds a chunk of Heights history covering the last hundred years.

The Brooklyn Historical Society in the heart of The Heights is where you go to find out about Herman Behr, Miss Middagh, or the conflagration in 1853 at General Underhill's landmark Colonnade, a row of eight wooden houses designed to resemble one antebellum Southern mansion, that went up in flames. The Historical Society contains over 125,000 volumes on Brooklyn (and Long Island). In the area of genealogy it's the third best in the country. Family his-

Walt Whitman's home while he was writing *Leaves of Grass* and working as an editorial writer on *The Brooklyn Daily Eagle*

tories and stories of old Brooklyn are researched here.

Love Lane—a tiny half street, an alleyway in The Heights—is it simply whimsy or history? To be accurate, history mixed with whimsy. Long ago two bachelor brothers by the name of De Bevoise lived in the house on the private lane with their adopted daughter—a scandalous business. Her admirers scribbled "love lines" to her on a fence. She eventually married and moved to Manhattan. The brothers grew strawberries in the backyard and played chess.

When the poet Hart Crane lived in The Heights in the late 1920s, he always wrote near a window with a view of the harbor. "There is all the glorious dance of the river . . . the skyline of Manhattan," he told a friend, "it is everything from the mountains to the walls of Jerusalem and Nineveh." The novelist John Dos Passos, who also lived nearby, frequently passed Crane tramping across the bridge late at night, usually in a drunken state. His patrons, the literary couple Harry and Caresse Crosby, who planned to publish *The Bridge*, were Crane's guests at a final bash in his Heights flat, with William Carlos Williams, e.e. cummings, Malcolm and Peggy Cowley, and some sailors and tattooed drifters from waterfront dives.

Hart Crane could not stay away from the notorious Sand Street area (now a housing project) near the Navy Yard. Many years later, around 1940, it provided Carson McCullers with the material for her

Garden Place Restoration in Brooklyn Heights. *Photograph © Tony Velez*

Rudolf Ivanovich Abel arriving for his espionage trial, August 8, 1957.
UPI/Bettmann

Cloak and Dagger, Fact and Fiction

On June 21, 1957, the FBI arrested Col. Rudolf Abel, a "master spy" who's believed to have operated the Russian espionage network in North America from an artist's studio in a building in Brooklyn Heights. Abel entered the United States in 1948, and, as a "cover," was a painter and photographer. He was known as Emil Goldfus, a passionate dabbler in social realism, to such artists as David Levine, Jules Feiffer, and Burt Silverman who also rented studios in the same building. His real talents were as a mathematician, radio engineer, and photographic technician. Sentenced to thirty years in prison, he was exchanged for Francis Gary Powers, the U2 pilot whose plane went down in the Soviet Union in the early 1960s.

Years earlier, in 1919, Christopher Morley used Brooklyn Heights as the setting for a fictional German spy ring in *The Haunted Bookshop*. Situated in a brownstone, near a main street of florists, tobacconists, and small modistes, the shop specializes in works by Carlyle, Emerson, Thoreau, Chesterton, Shaw, and Ambrose Bierce. A neighborhood German–American druggist, "one of the most dangerous spies," plans to bind an incendiary bomb into a doctored copy of Carlyle's *Oliver Cromwell* (a favorite of President Wilson's) and plant it in the president's stateroom before he sails to a peace conference. The pluckish bookstore owners thwart the villains. The bomb explodes inside their shop, shattering the fragrance of mellowed paper and leather. But they are not hurt. "Thanks to that set of Trollope," says the owner. "Books make good shock absorbers."

Truman Capote wrote the quintessential New York story *Breakfast at Tiffany's* while living in Brooklyn Heights. *Columbia University Libraries, Rare Book and Manuscript Library, New York*

Brooklyn Heights, the Esplanade.
Photograph © David Lee

novella *The Ballad of the Sad Cafe.* "In one bar, there is a little hunchback who struts in proudly every evening, and is petted by everyone, given free drinks, and treated as a sort of mascot by the proprietor," she once recalled.

Carson McCullers was then in The Heights at 7 Middagh Street, a forgettable address that attracted an unforgettable assortment of people. George Davis, the literary editor of *Harper's Bazaar,* had rented the house and invited McCullers to join him. (He had published a portion of her then-shocking work, *Reflections in a Golden Eye.*) Soon the tenants included W. H. Auden, Jane and Paul Bowles, and the stage designer Oliver Smith. Others who came for short visits were Anais Nin, Christopher Isherwood, Benjamin Britten, and Gypsy Rose Lee, who realized the group knew about music and literature but little about cooking. She hired as cook a former dancer from the Cotton Club. Anais Nin says that the house was like a museum of Americana. "Old American furniture, oil lamps, brass beds, little coffee tables, heavy dining tables of oak, grandfather clocks."

For McCullers, the Brooklyn experience made a lasting impression. "It is strange in New York to find yourself living in a real neighborhood." She knew the corner druggist; the man who sold coal; an Italian electrician who insisted she sup on provalone, cheese, salami, and pastries at his house; and an old lady who picked up stray, starving dogs. "Brooklyn, in a dignified way, is a fantastic place," she observed, and "there is always the feeling of the sea."

Truman Capote found Brooklyn Heights as "elegant and other-era as a formal calling card." And though parts of it were "rather doll pretty," invoking visions of bearded seafaring fathers and bonneted stay-at-home wives, he eagerly moved into the five-room basement apartment of a yellow brick house on Willow Street that belonged to Oliver Smith, who, after leaving the menagerie on Middagh, had multiplied his talents to producing shows and co-directing the American Ballet Theatre. Capote furnished the flat with mementos: a Fabergé pillbox, some marbles, bamboo bookcases, blue ceramic fruit, and paperweights. He had a Victorian "salon" and a kitchen with a yellow floor, but best of all, his bedroom opened onto a garden of wisteria and forsythia. In this setting of "sweet glimmerings recaptured," he wrote *Breakfast at Tiffany's.* Often a week went by without his "crossing the bridge" to Manhattan. When asked, "What do you *do* over there?" Capote replied that life could be fairly exciting. "Remember Colonel Rudolph Abel, the Russian secret agent? Know where they nabbed him? Right here!"

Above all, Brooklyn Heights has the Esplanade over the Brook-

lyn–Queens Expressway, giving strollers a magnificent view of sunsets. A playground on the northern end of the Esplanade is named after a neighborhood boy, Harry Chapin, the singer and crusader against world hunger who died in a car crash in 1981.

His brother Tom recalls: "Montague was once a wonderfully human street." "You knew the butcher, the baker, the shoe man. Now, only the big powers can survive. It's disturbing to see the mom-and-pop shops close, to be driven out by high rents." His fondest, most nostalgic memory is the school yard at P.S. 8, a half-block from his home. "There was a good racial and socio-economic mix. And the school yard was a tough proving ground, a very masculine place with a small-town feel. When it was time to go home, my mother could lean out our back window and yell, 'dinner.' It was a secure world." Chapin, who is six feet five inches, played basketball all over Brooklyn. "A guy on another team would say, 'I live in Flatbush or East New York, where do you live?' I'd answer, The Heights. Then he'd reply, 'Aw, that's not *real* Brooklyn—.'"

SUNLIGHT, SHADOWS, SWEAT

"—And when we wanted to see where the rich people lived, we'd go down to Brooklyn Heights." Danny Kaye, the tonsil-juggling clown whose rubbery arms and legs, google eyes, and manic smile provoked laughter in movie theaters around the world, was reminiscing about his youth in the neighborhood known as East New York. His audience was a summer crowd in Grand Army Plaza where Kaye, who entertained royalty at Buckingham Palace more often than any other American performer, had just been crowned the 1986 king of the borough's annual "Welcome Back to Brooklyn Day," a festival of eggs creams, Italian sausages, tropical fruit drinks, and cheesecake, along with marching bands, African drummers, jazz singers, and a turtle race. "I'm from Brooklyn and proud of it," announced the 73-year-old star, giving a poke in the ribs to social climbers who still don't realize that it's okay to be from Brooklyn. It's even chic.

East New York had been settled by old moneyed Dutch and British families. By the time Danny Kaye moved with his parents into a two-family house at 250 Bradford Street immigrants primarily from Germany but also from Italy and Russia lived close enough to each other to find out differences between Christmas and Hannukah, Easter and Passover. Kaye's parents came from the Ukraine where his father had been a horse dealer. When they settled in Williamsburg he became a tailor in a sweatshop.

Moving to East New York was a step up, and he had his own business. Williamsburg, Brownsville, and Greenpoint were bleak,

Danny and Sylvia Fine Kaye before they left Brooklyn for Hollywood, c. 1942–43. *Courtesy Sylvia Fine Kaye*

The soda fountain in the drug store, c. 1910. *Culver Pictures*

though not as despairing as Manhattan's Lower East Side. The next step up, and a fairly big one, too, was East New York, where the houses were comfortable and populated by doctors, dentists, lawyers, musicians.

Danny said he benefited a lot from being raised in East New York. "You learned it didn't make sense to dislike anybody because he was an Italian, a Jew, or an Irishman, or whatever. Although there were cultural differences, what counted was what you yourself were." With his singing and miming, he made everyone laugh.

But his specialty was playing hooky. Ultimately, he left school to travel with a vaudeville troupe through China.

As in small-town America, teenagers used candy stores as hangouts. Although the kids didn't know it, so did the treacherous Murder, Inc. that killed for money. "But you felt safe," recalls Kaye's wife, Sylvia Fine. "Girls went to the drug stores for sodas—remember the *soda fountain?*—but they also knew the boys were there. And the streets were safe. The girls played stoop ball and the boys played stick ball." She lived at the other end of Bradford Street in a brick single-family house surrounded by lilacs and rose bushes. Her father was a dentist. Years before, when his office was on Pennsylvania Avenue, members of Murder, Inc. came to him as patients. They were exceedingly polite. Dr. Fine wisely never charged the Mob for working on their incisors, or anything else.

The dazzlingly smart Sylvia Fine practiced the piano daily and later wrote parodies and comic sketches. She went on to write a Broadway show, then married Danny Kaye and dreamed up a series

Pentecostal Church Fuente de Vida Eterna in East New York. *Photograph © David Lee*

Minding the children in East New York *Photograph © David Lee*

of scintillating comedy numbers for a nightclub engagement that catapulted him into the musical *Lady in the Dark* (1941) and soon a film contract with Samuel Goldwyn. The mogul who's purported to have said, "Include me out," included Sylvia in. No fool he, Goldwyn gave her a contract, too, and she became a writer-producer. Her own favorite one-liner from her Brooklyn youth is ageless: "The great American tragedy is to have no date on sagedy." (This was the heyday of Ogden Nash.)

In East New York and then in Flatbush, she and her friends amused themselves with costume parties and treasure hunts. Taking the El downtown to the Brooklyn Paramount, now a part of Long Island University, they saw Fanny Brice do her burlesque of *Swan Lake* and heard Rudy Vallee, with a megaphone, warble "My Time Is Your Time."

The country was in the middle of the Great Depression. But it was also a time of simple, innocent pleasures. The borough erupted into laughter, and made news, when a seal waddled his way out of the zoo and proceeded down Flatbush Avenue. It was not in the middle of the night; it was during rush hour. "Nobody spotted him or paid any attention," remembers Sylvia, "until he wound up in a bar about two-and-a-half blocks from Prospect Park. Three drunks took one look and swore off."

After World War II, East New York was one of several neighborhoods that underwent dramatic demographic changes. Corrupt white and black realtors, with a speculative financial eye on the architectural splendors of Bedford–Stuyvesant, began "block busting"—sending a white to buy a house and then moving in a black family. Whites in Bed-Stuy, East New York, and Brownsville panicked. They fled to New Jersey and Long Island, reminding themselves that their childhood neighborhoods already had drug problems. It seemed inconceivable, in those innocent days, that drugs would follow them to the suburbs! And the Brooklyn that Danny Kaye remembered, where "you didn't dislike anybody," suddenly saw flare-ups of racial intolerance, bigotry, and terrible fear.

The federally funded Starrett City, a racially integrated housing complex built on Canarsie flatlands near East New York in the mid-70s, has over 15,000 residents living together compatibly today. But many Brooklyn leaders feel strongly that the answer for returning civility to neighborhoods is not the construction of enormous projects, but the restoration of row houses for single families, where a sense of individuality infuses more pride than the anonymity of super-sized apartment buildings.

Today, East New York is haunted by crime. It is fighting for its

life. In 1988 it had one hundred murder victims, higher than any other section in New York City. The mostly black and Hispanic residents of the 6.5-square-mile area see young people dealing drugs on sidewalks strewn with shattered glass bottles and garbage. One victim of the drug wars was a thirteen-year-old boy who had been shot once in a vacant apartment used by drug dealers. The police found glassine envelopes filled with cocaine and a 9-mm machine pistol.

There are no rosebushes anymore in East New York.

Brownsville probably never had flowers. Once a landscape of empty fields, in 1861 land there was purchased by Henrietta C. Brown to make a village. By 1886 Brownsville had five hundred small houses and a population of four thousand. In the 1920s it was settled by Eastern European Jews. But in more recent times it has come to represent urban streets of sorrow and squalor. At the turn of the century, the "nasty little slum" didn't even have sewers. But, with the completion of the Williamsburg Bridge in 1903 and a later subway that reached New Lots, it lured away from New York's teeming Lower East Side masses of poor Eastern European Jews.

Pretzel vendor in Brownsville.
Collections of the Municipal Archives of the
City of New York, W.P.A. Writers' Project

(The Williamsburg Bridge was known to some as the "Jews' Highway.") The literary critic and essayist Alfred Kazin, who grew up in Brownsville, recalls, "We were the end of the line. We were the children of the immigrants who had camped at the city's back door, in New York's rawest, remotest, cheapest ghetto, enclosed on one side by the Canarsie flats and on the other by the hallowed middle-class districts that showed us the way to New York." During the 1920s almost three hundred thousand cave dwellers experienced the chaotic tenement life of Brownsville where you needed wits and guts to survive. Day and night throngs jostled along Pitkin Avenue, the main street, exploring shops, restaurants, and a dreamland of

Overleaf

Pushcart Market on Belmont Avenue in Brownsville, 1910. *Photograph Underhill. The Brooklyn Public Library, Brooklyn Collection*

Shoeshine on Belmont Avenue, Brownsville. *Collections of the Municipal Archives of the City of New York, W.P.A. Writers' Project*

movies at the Pitkin Theatre, a furniture store today. On Belmont Avenue there were Yiddish playhouses and delicatessens with shining windows displaying a medley of kosher foods. Emerging from block after block of unpainted houses, frazzled housewives, who strove to keep together the body and soul of their families, carefully fingered fruits and vegetables at the Belmont Push-Cart Market. The open-air market still exists, but the vendors, once Jewish, are mostly black and Hispanic.

Political protest and reform movements were as much a part of daily life as the knishes and kreplachs. Socialists, Bolsheviks, atheists, and anarchists loudly declaimed their philosophies and panaceas in Zion Park on Friday nights. For a while the anarchist Emma

Goldman operated an ice-cream parlor, putting vanilla and strawberry scoops on cones while contemplating the abolition of government. The poverty of Brownsville inspired the crusader Margaret Sanger to open America's first birth control clinic at 46 Amboy Street in 1916. She envisioned families where children were *wanted*—and given every advantage. Tearful women told of their husbands' meager income (when there was work), of their helplessness in the struggle to make ends meet, of whining, sickly children, and the constant worry of another baby, year after year. A mother of eight, who also toiled in a sweatshop making hats, said, "If you don't help me, I'm going to chop up a glass and swallow it tonight." Sanger's clinic opened—and was closed by the vice squad nine days later. She was sentenced to thirty days in jail. Her controversial movement, starting with the desperate in Brownsville, brought a new freedom to women across America.

Emma Goldman speaking in Union Square, 1916. *UPI/Bettman*

Margaret Sanger on trial at the Court of Special Session. *UPI/Bettmann*

Muslim citizen street patrols on Amboy Street. *Photograph © David Lee*

Kids playing in the streets of Bedford-Stuyvesant. *Photograph © David Lee*

In the early 1980s the streets of Brownsville blazed in rioting and at least eight buildings were left in ruins in Amboy Street. The rat-infested rubble for some time had provided a backdrop for street gangs—The Amboy Dukes, for example, as early as the 1940s—and dope addicts. And Amboy Street was already rough when Mike Tyson—who later was to win the heavyweight boxing championship of the world—lived there as a kid. He also knew other danger zones, for his nomadic family shuttled around, from East New York to Williamsburg to Bedford–Stuyvesant. He learned to be savvy with criminals by the age of ten. Crime was simply a thrilling real-life entertainment. Plenty of other youths found the dark world of pickpockets, robbers, drug dealers, pimps, and gun-toting gangs a cool place to be. Today, youngsters growing up on Amboy Street, which now has a neighborhood center, raise their eyes in hope. A community garden has replaced a garbage heap. But change may take a long time. Violence, triggered by crack, often flares over seemingly nothing at all. Not long ago, a teenager named Pacquita squabbled with another teenage girl about the ownership of a dog. A short time later Pacquita was dead—stabbed in the chest outside her apartment. It wasn't even eleven o'clock in the morning.

Bedford–Stuyvesant, originally Dutch farmland, in the early nineteenth century had a small black community, Bedford Corners; it later developed into a middle-class suburban community, and gradually went through transitions as prosperous Jews who didn't have to suffer the blight of Brownsville mixed with or followed German, Irish, and Italian families. The prestigious Washington lawyer Joseph A. Califano, Jr., whose grandparents were Italian–Irish, was born in the neighborhood. (Califano was domestic troubleshooter for President Johnson and a cabinet appointee of President Carter.) Though Bed–Stuy long had a small black population, Lena Horne, who lived on Chauncy Street, remembers it as mostly white. The arrival of a new subway line in 1936 added to the racial mix. The train was soon honored in Duke Ellington's famous "Take the 'A' Train."

The Bedford–Stuyvesant Restoration Corporation, formed in the late 60s by Senator Robert Kennedy, is busily trying to renovate boarded-up, graffiti-scarred buildings in a community actively struggling against drugs. Students at St. John the Baptist School, a Roman Catholic elementary school, chased drug dealers away from an abandoned building used as a crack house and videotaped drug deals made nearby—sending copies of the tape to City Hall. Black professionals who've moved into spacious condominiums—with marble bathrooms and marble entrance halls—are angry that the

Brownsville Boy with Cheek

Lou Singer, a short, slightly rotund, *comfortable* fella, who was born some sixty years ago on the kitchen table ("My father always complained about Mom's cooking," he says with a mock-plaintive sigh), is a traveling encyclopedia of Brooklyniana. Today his popular mini-bus tours of the borough reveal a knowledge of nooks and crannies first discovered as a youth, growing up poor in Brownsville and exploring on foot winding roads, lanes, and streets. Some came to a dead end at Linden Boulevard, once tabbed Nanny Goat Boulevard, he recalls, because Italian farmers raised goats on the open fields. Others led to the silent-era Vitagraph Studios in Flatbush where Mary Pickford acted and had a house nearby. "I was a Jewish kid and knew that I had to take certain routes to keep from getting the hell beat out of me. On my wanders into the gentile world of Park Slope and The Heights, I noticed that the streets were empty. There were no people on stoops, calling and waving to each other. I imagined that behind lace curtains the occupants were whispering, 'What's he doing here?' "

The Singer family never had any money. His father, a skilled worker on men's clothing, was a compulsive gambler. "Sometimes my brother and I helped our mother clean buildings. We were harassed by loan sharks, so always on the move. My two sisters, my brother, and I loaded up a pushcart of kitchen tables and chairs—we had no couch—and settled on another street. But we never lived closer than two blocks to the El. It made a terrible noise."

At age twelve, Singer had a job as a delivery boy for rental tuxedo shops. "You didn't get paid. You made money from tips. If you were fast, you could earn about four dollars in fourteen hours. I also shined shoes, delivered papers and milk. And I read a lot. My mother said, 'How will you earn a living, all you do is read books. Your Uncle Morris, he's a poet, he can't earn a living,' and she'd weep. Then I discovered sex. A long subway ride to a girl's house wasn't a problem because you didn't worry about crime. The only thing I worried about was, will I get to smooch this time?"

He studied at City College and New York University, and eventually organized his own newspaper distribution company in Brooklyn. On his rounds, making home collections, he'd peer into houses with Tiffany windows and crystal chandeliers, then research their history. "I say to people, *look around!* There are people in this world who spend their life always looking in the road to avoid the dog droppings. Raise your eyes to the stars, say I, and if you step in some muck, the curb is there for your feet. But do not get trapped into lowering your gaze."

Lou Singer—a man who claims to know a thousand and one stories about Brooklyn. *Photograph © Benjamin Halpern*

53

The Birth of Philo Vance

Without the unsolved murder in 1920 of a popular auction bridge authority from Bedford–Stuyvesant, there'd be no Philo Vance detective series by S. S. Van Dine. The bizarre story of false teeth, toupees, monogrammed pajamas, and a bullet hole in the victim's head was the basis of Van Dine's first book, *The Benson Murder Case*.

Joseph B. Elwell grew up in the area around 1900 when many greystone and limestone houses had fine lawns and the Tomkins Avenue Congregational Church was a center of social activity (today, it's known as the First African Methodist–Episcopal Zion Church). Elwell was an enthusiastic church member who organized the Young Men's Club. Then cards became an obsession. He drifted away from the church. He even drifted away from Brooklyn. If he could earn his way at whist and bridge in Manhattan, why be a hardware salesman in the borough of hearty breakfasts?

Polishing his game and conversational graces, he married Helen Derby, who was several rungs up the social ladder. With his wife's encouragement he wrote *Elwell on Bridge*, an instant best-seller. As royalties from other bridge books followed, his income increased. So did his fondness for the stock market, horse racing, and the nymphs of Palm Beach and Newport, Rhode Island. When the couple separated in 1916, he was a millionaire.

A gambler with hearts and horses, he was found murdered in silk pajamas, at the age of forty-four, in his Manhattan town house. The police never discovered the weapon. They did discover that the boulevardier was completely bald and had only three teeth. Grieving mistresses had the vapors upon learning of his cosmetic deceits, and his teeth became the talk of the town. Who had Elwell let into his house without one of his forty toupees and teeth? Years later Alexander Woollcott hinted that his partner in the ownership of racehorses may have pulled the trigger.

Elwell's wife had the last word: "I introduced him into the best circles. When he made me a victim of his charms, he was nothing more than an obscure, handsome lad from Brooklyn."

Mourners at the funeral of Joseph B. Elwell, victim of an unsolved crime. *UPI/Bettmann*

rebuilding of their neighborhood is threatened by the drug menace. A single woman who began renovating a brownstone purchased from a private developer was killed by a crack addict six weeks after she started painting and sanding. Crack dealers who stalked Fulton Street were finally driven away by the police and Muslim patrols, but the dealers just moved onto residential blocks. It's a scary place to be at night or to wait for a subway. The same story is heard in Bushwick, which once had a sturdy German population that worked in the breweries, and still has remnants of mansions built for the beer tycoons. Out of fear, the residents—blacks, Hispanics, some whites—have taken a live-and-let-live attitude toward drug dealers. Red Hook, a once crumbling waterfront community where honest longshoremen tried to rid the union of racketeers—and inspired Arthur Miller's drama *A View from the Bridge*—brims with drugs even as small brick houses attract artists, eager to buy inexpensive homes before they're snapped up by realtors who foresee a gentrified neighborhood. Gangsters of different eras who walked

Children playing on the fire escape in Bedford-Stuyvesant. *Photograph © David Lee*

A grandmother with her two grandchildren in Bedford Stuyvesant. *Photograph © David Lee*

the cobblestone streets—Al Capone of the 20s and Joey Gallo of the 60s—would not be surprised to hear that eight people were shot in Red Hook on one night, but they'd never understand its simultaneous socio-economic upturn. Red Hook's inhabitants may not be seen after nightfall, although they're optimistic that someday they'll stroll under moonlit skies. Dreams do not die quickly in Brooklyn.

OCEAN BREEZES

Brighton Beach, a year-round resort between Coney Island and Sheepshead Bay, went from a cozy middle-class enclave of cottages and bathhouses to a tattered and sleepy seaside spa for the aging poor and welfare families. Then in the mid-70s, with the arrival of Russian emigrés, many of whom didn't speak English, the beach-front village became known as "Little Odessa by the Sea," an allu-

On the boardwalk at Brighton Beach.
Photograph © David Lee

Shirley Chisholm surprised Capitol Hill with a mind of her own. *UPI/Bettmann*

Bright Victory

One of the longest journeys in the world, wrote the editor-essayist Norman Podhoretz, who grew up in Brownsville, is from certain neighborhoods in Brooklyn to certain parts of Manhattan. An even longer journey leads from the black ghetto that Bed–Stuy had become in the 1960s to the spacious avenues of Washington, D.C. But Shirley Chisholm, the first black woman legislator elected to the New York State Assembly, in 1964, made that extraordinary trip and continued to represent segments of Bed–Stuy, Crown Heights, and Williamsburg until 1982. Chisholm, a resident of Bedford–Stuyvesant, won her congressional seat in 1968, the same year Martin Luther King was assassinated. "Some people find it very hard to pull the lever beside the name of a black," she once said, adding with a certain irony, "but I've always met more discrimination being a woman than being a black."

On Capitol Hill, the freshman Democratic representative balked at a seniority system that put her on the Agriculture Committee, an irrelevant place, she argued, for someone who came from a Brooklyn ghetto. She was reassigned to the Veterans Affairs and then the Education and Labor committees. A woman with a mind of her own, she irked her own constituents and many liberals when she visited Alabama's George Wallace in the hospital after he was shot, and then joined the 1972 "Stop McGovern" movement. Eventually, however, she earned the confidence of her party and sat on the House Rules Committee.

Chisholm lived as a child in Bed–Stuy and Brownsville (with some years in Barbados, which gives her a West Indian accent). Like many other poor families, hers had an apartment, for a time, over a candy store. On Saturdays she often sat on her fire escape and "giggled at the Jewish neighbors going in and out of the synagogue." This resulted in punishment. "Mother was a deeply religious person, and would not hear of making fun of anyone's religion." On Sundays, she and her sisters, each carrying a Bible, attended services at the English Brethren Church.

In the early 1940s she graduated from Girl's High School on Nostrand Avenue. She studied hard (her parents knew the value of education) and received scholarships to Vassar and Oberlin. But boarding costs were too high, so, instead, she went to Brooklyn College. Compromise, Shirley Chisholm learned at an early age, "is the highest of all arts."

sion to the Ukrainian port on the Black Sea. The Russian immigrants, numbering up to 30,000, cluster together in their own social clubs and bars, quietly play chess and checkers on the splendid boardwalk that faces one of the beaches closest to Manhattan, and one of the cleanest. They sell three kinds of caviar, mackerel, and whitefish from shops decorated in Russian lettering. When New Yorkers want to go slumming in summer, it's to the baking sands of Brighton Beach, with a stand-up picnic of moscovska salami, rye bread, and a spritzer before a dip in the sea, followed by an uninhibited stretch in the sun. On chilly wintry days, the boardwalk is a crowded promenade with emigrés named Vladimir and Betya, bundled up in old furs, who pause in sidewalk cafés for a shot of vodka, which warms their meanderings past snowy sands.

The Odessa restaurant in Brighton Beach. *Photograph © David Lee*

On weekend nights, a banquet-sized restaurant nightclub called The Odessa draws a motley international collection of art and theater celebrities who arrive in limousines. From other Brooklyn neighborhoods, Eastern Europeans in sequins and spangles arrive by subway. Seated at long tables for eight or ten, and speaking in a multitude of tongues, the revelers consume platters of cutlets, chicken in creamy mushroom sauce, rice pilaf with carrots and lamb, stuffed cabbage, eggplant in sour cream, dumplings filled with fruit—it doesn't stop until you signal the waiter, *No more!* Between the courses of soup and vegetables, and great gulps of seltzer or vodka, couples fling themselves around on a glitzy dance floor—wildly, madly, passionately. It's like taking a night boat from Helsinki to Leningrad, especially when the tables begin to tilt.

Brighton Beach is not all music and dancing and building of castles in the sand. There are occasional collisions of hate. A Holocaust survivor who'd lived in a boarding house for more than twenty years found a swastika inked on his door, apparently the work of a young Cuban down the hall. The symbolism of the swastika was too much for the elderly man whose black yarmulke and cheery smile were known to sitters along the boardwalk. Words were shouted, a tussle ensued, and soon the freed inmate of Auschwitz lay dead on the floor—stabbed with a pair of scissors. He stood up for what he believed in; he considered himself fortunate to have survived the horrors of a concentration camp.

But the personality of the community, with its valuable oceanfront, may be visibly altered as multimillion-dollar condominiums are planned to attract younger upscale people. The Russian immigrants and forgotten retired folk who can't make it to Florida will be pushed out if their wooden houses and apartments are demolished. The Brighton Beach Bath & Racquet Club, a landmark since 1919, with paddle tennis court, three swimming pools, and cabanas, may someday be replaced by apartments selling for up to $275,000. The club's members are dying or moving into nursing homes, explain the owners, so the baths will have to close anyway. At nearby Sheepshead Bay, where fishing boats head out to sea at 6 o'clock in the morning and return in the late afternoon with flounder and sea bass to sell to lines of landlubbers, the clam bars and tackle shops will also give way to town houses overlooking a floating restaurant and museum boat. Many residents of the Irish–Italian community worry that in a few years there won't be a fleet of tooting boats docked alongside rickety piers, that their fishing haven will have become a picturesque seaport for tourists.

Elizabeth Holtzman, the first woman in the city's history to be elected district attorney of Brooklyn, grew up near Coney Island. Fondly remembering the boats of Sheepshead Bay, the boardwalk at Brighton Beach, and the fresh salty air of the entire area, she says, "I campaigned on the boardwalk at night—its unpretentious liveliness is one of New York's best kept secrets." Holtzman misses the rural farms of her childhood in the early 40s where pigs and chickens were raised, but she adds that some places, such as Sea Gate, are amazingly the same.

Outsiders aren't allowed to pass the barred entryway at Sea Gate, a private waterfront community near Coney Island, unless they've first been cleared by guards at the gatehouse who act as doormen announcing visitors to residents. Surrounded on three sides by water, Sea Gate has restricted traffic since it was developed at the turn of the century. It's no Malibu Colony and never was, though some homeowners claim houses were designed by Stanford White (his

Elizabeth Holtzman, as a young girl.
Courtesy Elizabeth Holtzman

The Van Alen House in Sea Gate.
Photograph © David Lee

Houses in Bensonhurst decorated for
Christmas. *Photograph © David Lee*

name, accurately or not, is attributed to many sites in Brooklyn). The 7,000 dwellers, who carry photo-identification cards as a means of stemming crime, live mostly in duplexes or houses faded with age. What Sea Gate does have is a glorious backyard—the Atlantic Ocean and Gravesend Bay.

"Our safe little haven was turned upside down during the war years," wrote Beverly Sills, recalling her early years in Sea Gate. "Our house was right on the ocean and we'd see troop ships leaving for Europe every day." Sills had already been a smash with Major Bowes on radio and recorded one of the most famous singing commercials: "Rinso White, Rinso White, happy little washday song." She had a beau then who never rang the doorbell. He'd lurk outside her house and announce his presence by whistling the Rinso White ditty. Her father would ask if she was dating a boy or a bird.

While Sills was being courted by whistles and appearing on the soap opera *Our Gal Sunday*, a house unlike any other was being constructed in Sea Gate. William Van Alen, architect of the Chrysler Building, a skyscraper that used exposed metal as part of its conception, had designed a steel box-shaped model for cheap, mass-produced, "prefabricated" homes. The exterior was then sprayed with a white paint that made the steel resemble stucco. After World War II the designer's single unit idea was shelved for housing projects. A Secret Serviceman for President Roosevelt bought the unique Van Alen structure whose Bauhaus modernity stands out amid Sea Gate's more florid Victoriana. In the late 60s, Peter Spanakos and his wife, Niki, both guidance counselors for the Board of Education, acquired the villa for around $65,000. Today it would probably sell for almost $1 million. The house has a panoramic view of lower New York Bay.

The waters around Sea Gate are watched by the Shore Patrol for drug runners and merchant sailors who, upon entering the harbor, often hurl contraband overboard and then come back in small boats to dive for the illegal booty. "We own the streets of Sea Gate," says the community association, but the worldly waters have lent themselves to boat chase sequences that would leave the Keystone Kops breathless.

A GLOBAL EMBRACE

Christmas in Bensonhurst, Bay Ridge, and Dyker Heights is a glittering outdoor celebration of the holiday season. Though Asian-Americans, along with many Jews and elderly Scandinavian immigrants, live in these neighborhoods, you see on lawns and porches of Italian–American families a melange of angels, Santas, reindeer, elves, kings bearing gold, frankincense and myrrh, and Nativity scenes, fashioned from wood and plastic. Houses on the

tree-lined streets are further adorned with bright garlands of red, yellow, white, blue, and orange Yuletide lights, which transform ordinary one and two-family dwellings into magical Christmas castles. Some residents spend three months preparing displays that have over fifty "characters" (from the baby Jesus to an ensemble of carolers) and require ten thousand light bulbs. Christmas was always a time of big family get-togethers, recalls one "decorator" with a flock of angels dancing in his windows; it was a time of heavenly cakes and cookies and nutbreads at grandma's where glorious ornaments and strings of lights that sparkled like jewelry illuminated lives for a few weeks with feelings of cheer and good will toward all men.

Little seems to have changed in the provincial community of Bensonhurst since the 1950s when Jackie Gleason portrayed an opinionated bus driver who lived there in TV's "The Honeymooners." It's a setting of lawn chairs under metal porch awnings and houses with aluminum siding; of fig trees and herb gardens; of shops that sell espresso coffeepots and elaborate bridal gowns. It's where stickball is played in the street and where Sandy Koufax, known as the Man with the Golden Arm, lived when he was a pitcher for the Dodgers. Its insularity has given it a sense of safety—and also fear of outsiders. In the summer of 1989 the neighborhood seethed with tension after a black teenager was shot to death in an attack by a gang of white youths. But hate and defiance aren't limited to outbreaks in Bensonhurst, which most would describe as a stable community. Almost three years earlier a white youth was clubbed to death by young blacks on a deserted subway station platform in Crown Heights, a few miles northeast of Bensonhurst. No one was ever arrested for the crime and there was no massive protest. The innocent victim was a visitor from Australia. It has been said that both men died because they got off at the wrong train station in the wrong neighborhood.

Bay Ridge still has a reputation for being a Scandinavian suburb, and, indeed, King Olaf V of Norway honored the community with a royal visit in 1975. Some years later a twenty-year-old youth named Alexander Ruas, who left Stockholm to study photography in Manhattan, spent many days in Bay Ridge trying to find a feeling of his homeland. He went to the Swedish and Norwegian Church and snacked on ginger cookies and Swedish meatballs and sausages in two delis, but otherwise found that there wasn't much to remind him of Scandinavia. "I talked with people in their sixties and seventies whose children had moved away, who felt that the old Scandinavian community was dying out," says Ruas, whose mother lives in Stockholm but whose father, Charles, an author-translator, re-

The "Gingerbread House," built in 1917. *Photograph © David Lee*

Washington Cemetery on MacDonald Avenue in Bensonhurst. *Photograph © David Lee*

Norwegian-American folk dancers in Bay Ridge. *Photograph © Peter Norrman*

The late King Olav V of Norway at the Norwegian Christian Home in Bay Ridge, during a 150th anniversary celebration marking the first arrival of Norwegian immigrants, October 8, 1975. *AP/Wide World Photos*

sides in SoHo. "I feel totally Swedish, so there was a bond in being from the same place and we all enjoyed speaking our native language. It's sad to see that the Scandinavian heritage isn't being passed on."

Bay Ridge has luxury mansions along Shore Parkway, which runs under the Verrazano Bridge, but there's nothing anywhere in Brooklyn quite like the thatched "Gingerbread House" on 82nd Street and Narrows Avenue, a stone storybook fantasy, built for a shipping merchant in 1917, where Hansel and Gretel, clinging to each other, could hide from the wicked witch. Vietnamese, Hispanics, Greeks, and Irish have joined the international potpourri, mingling with the last of the butchers, bakers, auto repairmen, and antique-clock restorers from Scandinavia.

Syrians and Lebanese who make Atlantic Avenue (between Court and Hicks streets) a nostalgic bazaar from the *Arabian Nights*—beaded costumes for belly dancing, lutes and drums, brass lamp shades, embroidered tablecloths, backgammon sets— add the aroma of spices and dried fruits to their New World homes in Bensonhurst and Bay Ridge.

Towering above the skyline in Greenpoint is the dome of the Russian Orthodox Cathedral of the Transfiguration. The neighborhood, known today as Little Poland, is also home to St. Stanislaus Kostka Church where mass is given in Polish. When Lech Walesa, founder of the Solidarity movement in Poland, made his first trip to New York in 1989, the thousands of Poles who live in Greenpoint felt a bracing pride. Their ancestors first settled in Greenpoint in the nineteenth century where they toiled alongside Irish and Italian immigrants in the shipyards and oil refineries. It means, said a Polish priest, that we have people we can admire. For many Polish emigrés today, Greenpoint is their first address here. A quiet community with modest simulated brick and shingled houses, it has a low crime rate—probably because of its relative inaccessibility by mass transit.

Greenpoint in its heyday produced glass and pottery, but to millions its most famous natural resource was the "queen of sex," Mae West, who was born of Irish–German parents in the late 1890s. West claimed to remember picnics as a toddler in Prospect Park where "gentlemen and deer ran wild." To establish a theatrical persona, she honed her exaggerated sexual mannerisms by watching performers of her day: Bert Savoy's vamping as a female impersonator and Eva Tanguay's "anything goes" antics. But she added, "I was always careful how I looked. I wanted to make a good impression. When I was a kid in Brooklyn, I'd eat my dinner with a mirror by my plate." Her self-mockery and audacious humor ("An

The young Mae West does a vaudeville turn impersonating a male. *Theatre Arts Collection, Harry Ransom Humanities Research Center, University of Texas, Austin*

Overleaf
Russian Orthodox Cathedral of the Transfiguration of Our Lord, Greenpoint. Built in 1920. *Photograph © David Lee*

orgasm a day keeps the doctor away") were more Brooklyn than Broadway.

Bordering Greenpoint is the neighborhood of Williamsburg, a fashionable resort in the mid-1800s of hotels and beer gardens where society's crème de la crème—the Vanderbilts and Whitneys—frolicked. With the completion of the Williamsburg Bridge it soon became a blue-collar area for German and Irish families and then a crammed tenement district of Eastern European Jews. The garrulous erotic novelist Henry Miller lived with his German parents at 662 Driggs Avenue near a tin factory with soot-covered walls and a burlesque house called The Bum. The odors of sewer gas, stacked rawhides, and baking bread left a deep impression. "I was born in the street and raised in the street," he wrote. "In the street you learn what human beings really are—." He was not pleased by the invasion from lower Manhattan. "Soon the streets looked like a dirty mouth with all the prominent teeth missing, with ugly charred stumps gaping here and there, the lips rotting, the palate gone." And yet he added years later, "Coming from Brooklyn did me good. Why? Because it was international."

Flatbush is the area of Brooklyn most known to Americans, thanks partly to Hollywood movies of the 1940s. (Remember a feverish William Bendix in *Lifeboat* recalling his girlfriend back home?) Some of those movies were shown in Loew's Kings in Flatbush, a splendiferous 3,200-seat movie theater, now closed, de-

Nino Pantano, the "Boy Caruso" from Brooklyn, and winner of the A&S Contest in July 1949. *Courtesy Nino Pantano*

The "Caruso" of Carroll Gardens

When Nino Pantano was about ten years old, in the mid-1940s, he was touted as "the boy Caruso" of Brooklyn. He amazed relatives and friends, singing arias from *The Barber of Seville* and *Pagliacci*, and appeared on the "Paul Whiteman Show." But his parents weren't opera buffs—they didn't know what to do with him. He now works for the city and lives in Carroll Gardens, a colony of Italian, Irish, Swedish, and Middle Eastern immigrants, where young professionals are converting Romanesque churches into family apartments windowed in stained glass.

Over the years, Pantano collected rare Caruso records and memorabilia, including pictures of the tenor singing in Sheepshead Bay to raise money for World War I. When the Carroll Gardens Community Library asked Pantano to present an "Evening with Caruso" (lecture and music), he packed the house and later brought five hundred spectators to Carroll Park where he repeated his Caruso show.

Wearing a blue navy commander jacket, red tie, and white pants—"a kind of Pinkerton outfit from *Butterfly*"—Pantano sings "Come back to Sorrento" and then joins Caruso, on record, in other favorites. For the finale, with his son playing drums, he asks the audience to join him in George M. Cohan's "Over There," which Caruso sang in 1918. Amid singing, clapping, and emotional outbursts of weeping, Pantano marches through the crowd holding the Italian and American flags. "This is more fun than being *in* show business," he says.

Young Hasidic Jews in Williamsburg.
Photograph © Ted Beck

Henry Miller at age four

Man Ray with one of his designs for chessmen, c. 1942

Aaron Copland. *Museum of the City of New York, Theatre Collection*

signed to resemble a Beaux-Arts opera house. Flatbush has Victorian, Tudor, and Spanish-styled residences as ambitious as Loew's Kings where Barbra Streisand once ushered. There are also row houses and apartments, for Flatbush, which covers about three and one-half square miles in the center of Brooklyn, is a microcosm of the borough, a mix of the poor, the affluent, and the respectable middle class.

Ivan Karp, who owns the O.K. Harris Gallery in SoHo, grew up in Flatbush during the Depression. "It was a lovely place to live. Nobody could afford cars then, so you got around on foot, on roller skates, on the trolleys, or on bikes. I rode my bike through mountains of leaves in the fall. If you avoided hostile streets, you could ride your bike anywhere without fear." His father worked a sixteen-hour day in a haberdashery, and young Karp made hat deliveries after school. Life was dominated by the need for survival: how will we "get through" to payday next week? Homeowners were mostly Dutch, Irish, and German. The Italians and Jews, he says, lived in apartments but got along fairly well—"two temperamentally similar groups with intense family connections."

Before joining the army in 1944, Karp was the block air-raid warden. Describing himself as an authority on what German subs could see, he'd call out, "Mrs. Nussbaum, turn out those lights or subs will sink our ships!"

Bonjour, Paris

Heavy curtains drawn back to let sunlight into a hotel room, the sipping of chocolate and munching of croissants—Paris! It was exactly as Henry Miller imagined it when he left Brooklyn for Paris in the 1920s to transform himself into an artist and cosmopolite. Two other Brooklyn boys, soon to be world famous, also went to Paris around the same time. Emmanuel Radnitsky, the son of a Russian immigrant tailor, who grew up, as did Henry Miller, in Greenpoint, changed his name to Man Ray and became the first and most important of the American-born Dadaists (the word "dada" is French for a child's hobbyhorse and was chosen to show a contempt for rationalism). When Surrealism developed out of Dadaism in 1924, Man Ray—painter, avant-garde filmmaker, and photographer—was a key figure of the new movement. Remembering his youth—painting in solitude at Coney Island—he said, "I thought of myself as a Thoreau, breaking free of all ties and duties to society." Decades later, Man Ray, who used the materials of art to poke fun at serious ideas, added, "When you are sure of yourself, you can afford to be amusing."

Aaron Copland, who lived above his father's department store in Crown Heights, explored new musical sounds in Paris—Schoenberg, Stravinsky, Bartok—and then vitalized American music with the idioms of ragtime, jazz, and the blues. In two roaring cowboy ballets, *Billy the Kid* and *Rodeo*, Copland opened the musical West. His tender evocation of a pioneer wedding in *Appalachian Spring* demonstrates an ear for native rhythms that is unmistakably his own.

Baseball was critical to the well-being of everyone. "The Dodgers represented our joy and sadness." On Saturday afternoons, there was Loew's Kings—five hours of cinema that included a double feature, cartoons, a newsreel, a travelogue, and "coming attractions," and all for less than fifty cents.

Karp, who now lives in New York, visits Brooklyn frequently with his wife and children. Despite the physical decline of some neighborhoods, Karp feels "for the most part, Brooklyn hasn't changed. It doesn't have a horrid sense of suburban conformity. At its best, it has a modest, glowing tone and atmosphere."

MORE STATELY MANSIONS

Park Slope, which gently slopes away from Prospect Park and is near the grandeur of Brooklyn's own Arch of Triumph, is called the "Gold Coast." Within walking distance to the Brooklyn Museum, the Botanic Garden, and the main Brooklyn Library, it was established by, among others, Edwin C. Litchfield, the railroad tycoon; George Tangeman, the baking-powder millionaire; Charles L. Feltman, the "hot dog" king; and Henry Carlton Hulbert, the paper tycoon.

Designated a historic area in 1973, Park Slope abounds in opulent mansions and town houses that evoke the ambience of Neuilly, outside Paris. Residents are fiercely proud of what one urban planner describes as "the most beautiful Victorian area on the East Coast, and probably in the United States." The houses—Gothic, Romanesque, Italianate—now duplexes and apartments, retain their turn-of-the-century appeal—original gas fixtures, marble sinks, stained-glass windows, wood paneling, fireplaces, chandeliers, and drawing rooms with parquet floors. Wine bars, new neighborhood hangouts that serve frothy drinks and sesame chicken wings, and gourmet take-out shops where Madison Avenue executives can buy soups and salads for slimming dinners at home further define today's Park Slope "personality."

That tall, regal woman on the street, hailing a taxi, who looks vaguely like a Brontë heroine, is really Dame Joan Sutherland, who lives on the Slope with her husband, Richard Bonynge. A passing jogger stops to say hello and discusses a Sutherland recording. Soon a young mother pushing a baby carriage exchanges a friendly greeting. Sutherland has lived in Brooklyn for twenty years. "I first had an apartment in Greenwich Village, but it was getting too hectic there. Park Slope gets me away from the rush of Manhattan, it's very homey and has a Parisian feeling." The lyric-coloratura, one of the greatest singers of the century, also has residences in her native Australia and Switzerland. "Some friends in Manhattan were

A youthful Ivan Karp, now owner of the O. K. Harris art gallery in SoHo, New York. As a kid in Brooklyn, he was an air-raid warden who warned, "Mrs. Nussbaum, turn out your lights!"
Courtesy Ivan Karp

shocked that we added Brooklyn as our American residence, but they've never really been here. I love driving home over the bridge and looking back at the skyscrapers of Manhattan."

But, as Park Slope becomes one of the hottest real estate markets in Brooklyn, mean-spirited beatings and an increase in drug-related crimes have made triple locks, alarm systems, and protective dogs a necessity. In some areas of the Slope, residents pay $30 a month for private patrols from late afternoon until dawn. Everyone agrees that crack is casting a pervasive shadow on the Slope and, as one member of the community put it, "Today the anxiety level is overwhelming."

Fort Greene, another landmark district with fine Queen Anne and French Empire row houses (some built by Walt Whitman when he was a carpenter), reflects a fondness for London: the streets are named Adelphi, Carlton, and Oxford. The poet Marianne Moore, "a staunch Brooklynite," lived and wrote for most of her life across from Fort Greene Park at 260 Cumberland Street. A familiar figure in her flowing cape and tricorn hat, Moore remained there for over thirty years—until friends, worried about the neighborhood's decay in the 1960s, urged her to find a safer address, which she did in Greenwich Village. However, she confided, "You know, I always keep a gun in my desk." That was long before the renaissance of brownstones in Fort Greene, which sell today for $300,000.

"Brooklyn has given me pleasure, has helped educate me; has afforded me, in fact, the kind of tame excitement on which I thrive," she once said, recalling the days when a neighbor in "calling costume, furred jacket, veil and kid gloves" went grocery shopping on Myrtle Avenue. A member of the Lafayette Avenue

Entrance of the Thomas Adams residence, with a massive arch supported by Romanesque-capped columns. *Photograph © David Lee*

Things That Go Bump in the Night

Thomas Adams, Jr., the rajah of chewing gum, built a mansion at 115-119 Eighth Avenue, on the northeast corner of Carroll Street, in 1888. According to legend, it was among the first private houses to have an elevator—a sort of gilded birdcage contraption. In the summer of 1894, the Adams family left Park Slope for their second home on the north shore of Long Island. When they returned in the fall, the Carroll Street house was dark and quiet. They rang for the servants, but there was no response. They entered the house and rang for the elevator, but it didn't come.

While the family was away, the legend continues, the elevator became stuck between floors. Four servants, trapped inside, were found dead. Eventually, the vast house was sold, divided into apartments, and the elevator removed. But some of the apartments had bedroom alcoves in what had been the elevator shaft. Years later, tenants—unaware of the story—allegedly complained of nightmares in which they heard Irish-accented voices crying, *"Water—food—Mary, Mother of God, help us!"* The legend ends on a practical note: no one sleeps in the alcoves anymore.

Dame Joan Sutherland, who makes her American home in Park Slope.
Photograph © Christian Steiner

Presbyterian Church, she'd be pleased to know that today it's the site of Handel and Scarlatti concerts by The Brooklyn Friends of Chamber Music. Of her community she said, with the precision—and brevity—of her poetry: "I find it quite dear to me."

Three blocks from the Pratt Institute, where Clinton Hill and Fort Greene merge, is a row of carriage houses where the wealthy folks who lived on "The Hill" once kept their horses and broughams and servants. Across the street three mansions were demolished during World War II and replaced by a navy officers building, now a community housing project. George McNeil lives behind a steel, seemingly bulletproof door in one of the brick carriage houses. A figurative and abstract expressionist for over sixty-two years, the Brooklyn-born painter grew up in a working class family that emigrated from Ireland in 1850. For the last twenty years he and his wife have lived in Brooklyn by choice. What he sees as the aridity of SoHo does not interest him. His work celebrates life and energy and the ethnicity of his neighborhood. He captures disco-dancing punksters in goofy costumes, sporting bizarre hairdos, who visit shops that sell voodoo dolls, elixirs and powders, and votive candles. It's the frenzy of a different world where noise and ritualistic potions attempt to shut out unhappiness. "This is a semi-stable neighborhood today, but you don't go out alone after dark. And it's a nervous environment for kids. If they show intellectual curiosity, they get beaten up. What do you do with the poor who have an aversion to learning? Crime, I believe, festers, in the big housing complexes. Renovating smaller houses is a much saner concept. Now, the kind of people who fled to the suburbs thirty years ago want to live here. It can only improve the neighborhood, keep it from becoming a threatening ghetto. The question is often asked, 'Who can really *know* Brooklyn?' It changes so often, maybe nobody can."

Gables, Dormers, Chimneys

LOVELY TO LOOK AT

Compared with Manhattan and its glamorous skyscrapers, Brooklyn seems—on the surface—like a dowdy poor relation. But the truth is that, during its more than three hundred fifty years of existence, the borough has actually become one of America's greatest living architectural museums. For starters, it has two of the world's most beautiful suspension bridges, the Brooklyn and the Verrazano Narrows. It has a park and two boulevards planned by the great nineteenth-century landscapists Frederick Olmstead and Calvert Vaux. It has a war memorial on Grand Army Plaza that is a compelling version of the Arc de Triomphe in Paris. It has a splendid Beaux Arts museum that houses one of the country's finest art collections. It has the Esplanade, an elevated walkway on the river that commands a dazzling view of Manhattan and its harbor. And it has what must certainly be the liveliest—architecturally speaking—cemetery in the country: Green-Wood, whose flamboyant Gothic Revival gates guard quaint Victorian tombs that evoke the mansions once occupied by the living.

But spectacular as these public facilities are, it's as "a borough of homes and churches" that Brooklyn expresses its real architectural character. Hundreds of charming, tree-lined blocks, in such neighborhoods as Brooklyn Heights, Park Slope, Carroll Gardens, Fort Greene, and Clinton Hill, contain some of the finest examples of these structures in America. In Brooklyn Heights, for instance, New York City's first suburb, and one of the loveliest urban residential neighborhoods in the world, there still stands a pair of stately Renaissance Revival mansions at numbers 2 and 3 Pierrepont Place, dating from 1857 and cited by the American Institute of Architects as "the most elegant brownstones left in New York." (A third was demolished in 1946; the site is now a playground.) The political reformer Seth Low, mayor of Brooklyn in the 1880s and later mayor of Greater New York, grew up in Number 3 Pierrepont

Originally, St. Ann's Episcopal Church, built in 1869, and now the auditorium of Packer Collegiate Institute.
Photograph © David Lee

75

Place. The other was occupied at one time by Alfred Tredway White, a businessman and philanthropist who, elegantly housed himself, built highly livable low-rent projects for working people, still standing in the Heights and Cobble Hill.

The Heights, with its spectacular view of New York Harbor, offered a haven to prosperous Manhattan-dwellers who wanted closeness to the city without its bustle. Its history as a residential community began after Robert Fulton's fast steam ferry, *Nassau*, began regular service between Manhattan and Brooklyn in 1814. Seeing the lucrative possibilities, ambitious Heights landowners—the Pierreponts, the Hickses, the Joralemons—began dividing their properties into 25-by-100-foot building lots. The first concentration of row houses—mostly frame with a few brick examples—began around Hicks and Willow streets. Eventually, the Heights achieved fame for some of the most imposing residences in the Greater New York area, and until the close of the nineteenth century it remained primarily an area of residences and fine churches, along with private schools, clubs, and a few elegant hotels.

SETTING THE STYLE

As the days of Dutch Colonial architecture—with its low ceilings and overhanging roofs—waned, the Heights and other Brooklyn neighborhoods became a virtual encyclopedia of the successive architectural modes that America loved: Federal; the revival styles of Greek, Gothic, Romanesque, and Renaissance; Italianate, Venetian Gothic, and Queen Anne. Such distinguished architects as Richard Upjohn, James Renwick, Jr., Alexander Jackson Davis, and Minard Lafever came to the borough to build. Upjohn's contributions include the Church of the Pilgrims, 1846 (now Our Lady of Lebanon Maronite Cathedral). The church, in a Romanesque Revival style radical for its day, may have been the first such building in the country. It's a solid mass of stone, noted for its starkly simple tower and a later Art Deco touch: metal door panels from the liner *Normandie* that burned and sank in the Hudson River in 1942.

Renwick, the architect of St. Patrick's Cathedral in New York and the Smithsonian Institution in Washington, produced the ebullient St. Ann's Protestant Episcopal Church, 1869, in downtown Brooklyn, a Ruskinian Gothic behemoth with two spires and a façade enriched by the differing colors and textures of its stone. Minard Lafever, a carpenter-turned-designer, whose building guidebooks greatly influenced the widespread American fancy for classical revival, gave the Heights several fine structures in Gothic Revival style. Among them are the Packer Collegiate Institute, 1854, at 170 Joralemon; a seminary for young ladies that resembles a

House at 24 Middagh Street, in the Federal style, formerly the Eugene Boisselet residence, built in 1824.
Photograph © David Lee

Brooklyn Borough Hall, formerly the Brooklyn City Hall, built in 1846–51. *UPI/Bettmann*

The most elegant brownstones remaining in New York, Numbers 2 and 3 Pierrepont Place, between Pierrepont and Montague streets. Originally, they were the Alexander M. White and Abiel Abbot Low residences, built in 1857. Alfred Tredway White was born and brought up at Number 2. *Photograph © David Lee*

House at 70 Willow Street, formerly Adrian van Sinderen residence, built c. 1839. *Photograph © David Lee*

delightful Victorian castle, and at 157 Montague Street, the Diocesan Church of St. Ann and the Holy Trinity, 1847, now headquarters of the Episcopal Diocese of Brooklyn. Its dark-red brownstone exterior is badly weathered, but the interior is cast and painted terra cotta, a departure from the usual carved stone, with windows designed by William Jay Bolton, one of the foremost stained glass artists of the period. Unfortunately, St. Ann's lost its needlelike spire early in the century when blasting for a subway tunnel necessitated its dismantling.

Of the 1,100 houses still standing in the Heights, more than 600 were built before 1860. One of the earliest—and architecturally purest—is the house at 24 Middagh Street, dating from about 1820–24 and sometimes referred to as "The Queen of Brooklyn Heights"; it was formerly the Eugene Boisselet house. Built of wood and faced in clapboard, with a gambrel roof and a basement of brick, it has a small cottage connected by a garden wall. It's a beautifully preserved example of the light, elegant, and symmetrical Federal style, an American adaptation of English Georgian brought over here around 1790. But the truly great Federal-style residence in Brooklyn is the palatial Commandant's House in the Brooklyn Navy Yard, completed in 1806 and noted for its refinement of detail—the delicate columns and balusters of its porch, the arched tracery of the narrow dormer windows. The house is attributed to the Boston architect Charles Bulfinch, famed for his work on the Capitol in Washington, D.C.

Greek Revival, which swept through America beginning around 1820 and lasted for forty years, was not ignored in Brooklyn. Inspired by the classical, human-scale architecture of early Greece, the style conveyed the vigor of an ancient democracy to a worshipful new one. At once grand and simple, romantic and rational, it fit perfectly the optimistic, idealistic outlook of a young country expanding from sea to sea. Its hallmark was the columned portico, appearing on houses and public buildings alike. Greek Revival was obviously the ticket for Brooklyn's new seat of government, Borough Hall, designed by Gamaliel King—a former grocer and carpenter—and built between 1846 and 1851 on a triangular plot of land in what's now downtown Brooklyn. Its north front boasts a large Greek Ionic portico, set on a steep flight of steps and rising three stories high. Eventually, this politician's palace was crowned with an iron cupola (completed in 1898), a fussy Georgian hat that affronts its fine Greek presence.

The Greek Revival style translated well in residential terms, too. In the Heights, a fine stand of such houses, in painted brick and brownstone, with pedimented door frames and recessed doors flanked by pilasters, occurs on Willow Street, numbered 20 through 26 (Henry Ward Beecher, the famed first minister of the Plymouth Church, lived in No. 22). Another interesting example is the big three-story brick house at 70 Willow Street, four bays wide, with a pilastered doorway of brownstone and, inside, a circular stairway placed laterally in the hall. Once owned by a prosperous burgher, Adrian Van Sinderen, it's now the home of producer, set designer, and co-director of the American Ballet Theatre, Oliver Smith. "I've lived in Brooklyn since 1939," says Smith. "What appeals to me is the nineteenth-century quality of the architecture. The use of brick, much of it imported from Holland, reminds me of areas in Baltimore and Philadelphia. Brooklyn did not destroy its wonderful houses, so it has an *intimate* scale. It's not like living in a huge city."

In nearby Cobble Hill, the De Graw mansion at 219 Clinton Street, set on a beautifully landscaped plot overlooking the river, is

The DeGraw Mansion on Clinton Street, built in 1845 for the merchant Abraham DeGraw. *Photograph © David Lee*

79

Jennie Jerome, later Lady Randolph Churchill. *The Brooklyn Public Library, Portrait Collection*

Caroline Ladd Pratt house, now a Pratt Institute foreign-students dormitory. *Photograph © David Lee*

Residence of the Roman Catholic bishop of Brooklyn, built in 1893, formerly the home of Charles Millard Pratt. *Photograph © David Lee*

St. Joseph's College, formerly the Charles Pratt residence, built in 1875. *Photograph © David Lee*

an even more imposing example of Greek Revival. It was built in 1845 for the merchant Abraham De Graw. When remodeled and enlarged nearly fifty years later by its second owner, it gained a stepped gable roof and a high tower fitted out with one of the first residential elevators in Brooklyn. True, the house has lost some of its Greek Revival character, but as the only free-standing home left in Cobble Hill, it's still an eye-stopper. Not far from here, on Amity, near the corner of Court Street, is the Greek Revival-style house where Jennie Jerome, mother of Winston Churchill, was born in 1854. (The façade has, alas, been bastardized with fake stone.) Jennie's father, Leonard, was a financier and horse lover, who constructed Jerome Avenue in the Bronx as a direct route to his race course.

But perhaps the finest Greek Revival house in the city is the beautifully preserved dwelling of salmon-colored brick at 440 Clinton Street in Carroll Gardens. Built around 1840, it rises three stories, with a façade flanked by full-height pilasters that are topped by stone capitals. This elegant mansion has not lost too much face in its present role as a funeral home, since its appearance is proudly kept up by its owners, the Guido family.

VILLAS, CHATEAUX, MANOR HOUSES

From the 1840s on, more romantic styles proliferated in Brooklyn—Gothic Revival, Romanesque Revival, Italianate, and Renaissance Revival among them. The Heights was teeming with them, and so was Clinton Hill, a residential area almost as desirable as the Heights. Charles Pratt, made a millionaire by his kerosene refinery, the Astral Oil Company, built a clubby group of family mansions on Clinton Avenue, known as the Fifth Avenue of Brooklyn. Three of them were wedding gifts for his sons. His own, at 232 Clinton Avenue, a manor house built in an Italianate style in 1875—now occupied by St. Joseph's College—is big but not nearly as distinctive as the one at 241 Clinton built for his son Charles Millard Pratt nearly twenty years later. Designed by William B. Tubby in "Richardsonian" Romanesque, it is notable for a fine arched porte-cochère that holds within its curve both the entrance to the house and its carriageway. At the opposite side a kind of asymmetrical balance is struck by a semicircular conservatory. Though it could be a parsonage in a Trollope novel, it is now occupied by the Roman Catholic bishop of Brooklyn. The two other Pratt houses are Georgian Revival in style, and less literary looking.

The biggest and most varied preserve of romantic styles is Park Slope, a gentle rise of land from the Gowanus Canal to what is now

The Woodward Park School, at 50 Prospect Park West, originally the Henry Hulbert residence, built in 1883.

Photograph © David Lee

Prospect Park. Before the century turned, the area had so many spectacular houses it was known as Brooklyn's Gold Coast. The granddaddy of them all was the Litchfield Villa, built in Italianate style in 1857, almost a decade before the development of Prospect Park—and now surrounded by it. It was designed as the home of Edwin C. Litchfield, a lawyer and railroad developer, by Alexander Jackson Davis, one of the foremost architects of the mid-nineteenth century. The mansion, a splendid massing of towers, balconies, turrets, bay windows, and porches, was richly furnished inside and for years served as a gathering place for Brooklyn society. In the 1860s, the city bought some of Litchfield's property (he owned virtually all of what's now Park Slope) to help form Prospect Park. Today, the mansion is occupied by the Brooklyn office of New York City's Department of Parks and Recreation, and it has been sadly stripped of its finery, including the stucco façade. Still, it's a very visible relic of Brooklyn's age of opulence.

But a magnificent limestone pile nearby at 50 Prospect Park West, built for a paper tycoon in 1883, retains its original presence even though it currently houses the Woodward Park School. Designed by Montrose Morris, a prolific local architect, in the Romanesque Revival style, this massive structure, with its roof line

vigorously punctuated by towers, gables, chimneys, and dormer windows, suggests both a fortress and a French château. At the time it was built, it had an unobstructed view of the harbor. It's in good company, since many of its peers still stand, among them the residence on Eighth Avenue built in 1888 for Thomas Adams, Jr., the chiclet millionaire, designed by Charles P. H. Gilbert and considered the finest Romanesque Revival house in the city. As grand a palace as can be crammed onto a double city lot, the house is a skillful orchestration of carved and textured masonry—brick, sandstone, brownstone, and terra-cotta. Its most striking features are a massive Richardsonian entrance arch and a mammoth corner tower that turns from round to angular as it rises above the first story. Alas! Twentieth-century economics have turned the house into a multifamily dwelling.

The villa built in 1857 for Edwin C. Litchfield, now the Brooklyn headquarters of the New York City Department of Parks in Prospect Park. The Brooklyn Public Library, Brooklyn Collection

METROPOLITAN HOMES

There were creative real estate developers in Brooklyn who scorned the cookie-cutter approach to urban housing. Montgomery Place, a stage set where turrets, gables, odd-angled windows, and picturesque doorways take one from Brooklyn to Belgravia, is one of the most extraordinary urban experiences in America. It was put up

between 1888 and 1904 by one Harvey Murdoch, who gave the ordinarily stuffy architect Charles P. H. Gilbert a free hand at creating a "master plan." Gilbert did twenty of the forty-six houses on the block, including No. 11, with a Dutch stepped gable, where Murdoch himself resided. The result is a model of town residential planning that survives as a monument to this unusually imaginative developer.

Another creative real estate man, Dean Alvord, made Flatbush the home of the first planned suburban community. Known as Prospect Park South, and conceived as an "urban park" in a rural setting, the area comprises some fifteen blocks of single-family mansions on broad, shaded plots that might serve as settings for lavish lawn parties. Alvord was out to interest "people of intelligence and good breeding" in his homes. He laid out wide streets—some with malls—and created the illusion of grand boulevards by planting trees every 20 feet at the property line just inside the sidewalk. Many of the homes, designed in adaptations of earlier styles—such as Greek Revival—were actually built between 1899 and 1910 and have still retained their original one-family status. (The shocking-pink house in the movie *Sophie's Choice*—originally an English gray—was found here, and has now been restored to its conservative color.) In this gracious, old-fashioned environment, removed from the urban hassle, one can almost imagine that the banker's son might return the prom queen to her house next-door at a highly respectable hour.

BLUE-COLLAR COTTAGES

Even for the less affluent, Brooklyn provided well. It has more than its share of slums, immortalized in movies and memoirs, but at the same time good affordable housing is part and parcel of the borough. Even gentrified Cobble Hill still has a place for the workingman. It is the site of one of the earliest low-rent complexes in the country. The "model tenements" known as the Warren Place Workingmen's Cottages, and the adjacent Tower and Home Apartments were put up in the late 1870s by Alfred Tredway White, a businessman whose slogan was "Philanthropy plus 5 percent." It was his way of saying that he could provide livable quarters for the poor at very low rentals and still make a profit. His visionary idea for tenement reform was inspired by a visit to the slums of London, as well as Walt Whitman's plea to philanthropists to build low-rent housing. The success of White's projects made even more shameful the squalid "old-law" tenements that continued to be erected by greedier developers.

Apartment building of salmon-colored brick on Clinton Street in Carroll Gardens. *Photograph © David Lee*

A mansion on Montgomery Place. *Photograph © David Lee*

Susan Smith McKinney Stewart, New
York's first black woman physician. *The
New York Public Library, Astor, Lenox
and Tilden Foundations, Schomburg Center
for Research in Black Culture*

The Bethel Tabernacle African
Methodist Episcopal Church, built in
1847. *The Metropolitan Museum of Art,
New York, Weeksville Society*

The forty-four brick "workingmen's" cottages, built at a cost of $1,150 each around a gardened walkway between Warren and Baltic streets, are very small but as charming as an English mews. In their time, these six-room dwellings rented for $18 per month. Today they are all privately owned, and change hands at six-figure prices. The nearby Tower and Home Apartment buildings originally provided nearly two hundred and fifty walk-ups—with indoor plumbing, rare for those days—for working people, each amply supplied with fresh air and sun by the innovative use of outside balconies and open stair towers. The buildings, on Hicks, Warren, and Baltic streets, are grouped around gardened courtyards meant to provide recreational space for the tenants. Rent for a four-room apartment at the time was a not-unaffordable $7 a month. The apartments were completely redone in 1979, with the help of a government subsidy.

White actually put up more than half a dozen such projects around Brooklyn, but the only other one standing today is the Riverside Apartments at 4–30 Columbia Place, designed by William Field and built in 1890. Due to the construction of the Brooklyn–Queens Expressway in the 1950s, however, only one of the buildings is left, with a remnant of the original garden. Not to be outdone in the area of benevolent patriarchy, in 1886 Charles Pratt also built a workers' housing project not far from his Astral oil refinery in Greenpoint. Designed in Queen Anne style, with balconies and cross-ventilation to provide light and air, this big, bold red-brick pile occupies the entire block on Franklin Street between Java and India streets. But today, in contrast to the Tower apartments in Cobble Hill, the place has the look of a nineteenth-century sanitarium, a look intensified by the sealing of its arched entryways. Obviously, that's to keep out muggers and mischief-makers.

Modest Miracle

Blacks had their own independent housing development. It was called Weeksville. This small cluster of modest frame dwellings that survive in the Crown Heights section of Brooklyn belonged to one of the earliest free black communities in the city. It dated from the 1830s. Only four of the houses—rediscovered in the 1960s on Bergen Street between Rochester and Buffalo avenues—are still standing, but they have been carefully restored as showplaces. Weeksville got its name from James Weeks, a black stevedore from Virginia who bought land in 1838, eleven years after slavery was legally abolished in New York state. The original settlers are thought to have been thirty or forty relatively prosperous black families, and the community remained predominantly black until after the Civil War. It produced a number of leading citizens, among them Susan Smith McKinney Stewart, New York's first black woman physician, who was born here in 1847.

PUBLIC PLACES

Though Brooklyn's architectural glory is its rich array of homes and churches, the borough is not lacking in distinguished structures of a more public nature. The genius of Frederick Olmstead and Calvert Vaux, who designed Prospect Park, also gave Brooklyn Grand Army Plaza. The area, with its stately sweep of boulevards, buildings, and greenery, brings to mind the grandeur of Paris. The oval plaza's centerpiece is the Soldiers' and Sailors' Monument, a triumphal arch completed in 1892 as a memorial to the Union forces in the Civil War. Designed by John H. Duncan, the architect of Grant's Tomb, the arch is topped with a traditional bronze quadriga—a horse-drawn chariot with a triumphal female figure, flanked by two winged victories. The work is by Frederick MacMonnies, a Brooklyn resident and a fine sculptor trained by Augustus Saint-Gaudens. Inside the arch are bas-reliefs depicting Lincoln, by Thomas Eakins, and Grant, by William O'Donovan.

Nearby, on or close to Eastern Parkway, are three great Brooklyn institutions: the Brooklyn Museum, the main branch of the Brooklyn Public Library, and the Brooklyn Botanic Garden. As it stands today, the museum, designed by Charles Follen McKim and

Prospect Park entrance at Grand Army Plaza. *Museum of the City of New York*

GRAND ARMY PLAZA at ENTRANCE to PROSPECT PARK BROOKLYN

Left
Calvert Vaux. *The Brooklyn Public Library, Portrait Collection*

Right
Frederick Law Olmsted in the late 1880s. *The Brooklyn Public Library, Eagle Collection*

Design for Prospect Park by Olmsted and Vaux

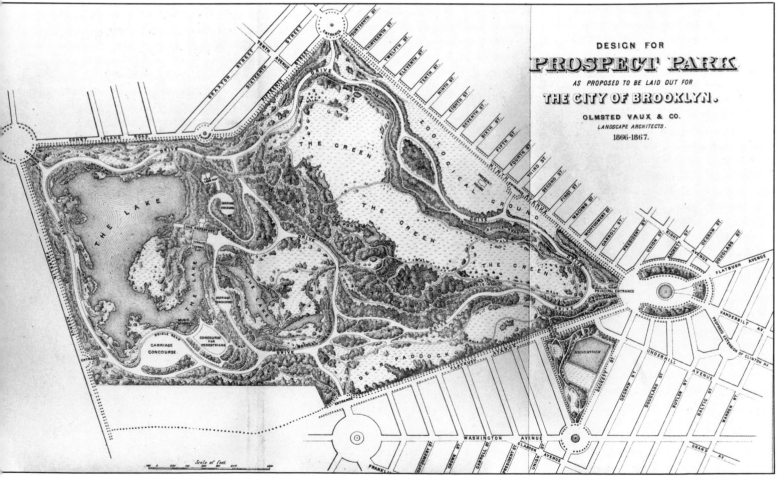

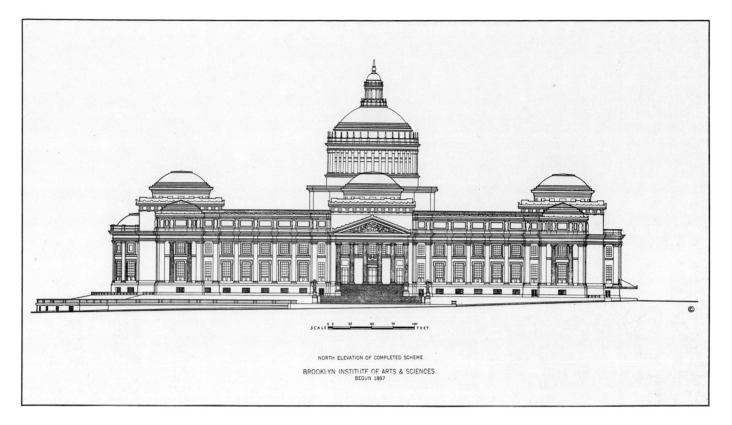

opened to the public in 1897, comprises only a portion of a far larger project. With Brooklyn's change from a city to a borough of Greater New York, funds to complete the grand concept simply vanished. But what did get built is nothing to sneeze at—a Beaux Arts extravaganza of noble proportions, at least viewed from the front (the building's hind quarters were never really completed). Behind the museum, and flanking the eastern end of Prospect Park, is the Botanic Garden, famous for its Japanese landscape garden. A recent $17-million program restored its Italian Renaissance-style administration building, a two-wing affair joined by a rotunda with a cupola on top, designed by McKim, Mead & White and completed in 1917. The very fin de siècle Palm House, a stately structure of glass and steel, has been made into a reception center, and there's a new huge conservatory, which, for all its geometric modernity, is still in harmony with the garden's Victorian character.

In contrast to the Beaux Arts splendor of the museum and the Botanic Garden is the Art Moderne Brooklyn Public Library, directly across from Grand Army Plaza. First planned in 1897, it took the city, what with one thing and another, more than fifty-six years to finish. Though it was opened to the public in 1941, behind the gold-leafed glass and limestone of the façade, more than half of the interior was still incomplete. Finished in the 1950s, the streamlined façade of the library makes an interesting counterpoint with the ornate exterior of the museum next door.

North elevation of the completed scheme of the Brooklyn Institute of Arts and Sciences (now the Brooklyn Museum) by McKim, Mead & White. *New-York Historical Society*

BANKS, CLUBS, HOTELS

As a city of homeowners, Brooklyn never developed anything like the density of commercial towers that crowds the Manhattan skyline. Unlike Manhattan, the sprawling borough never had to grow upward for lack of ground room. So its own high rises are all the more visible. The only building that sort of scrapes the sky, in the Manhattan sense, is the Williamsburgh Savings Bank Building, at One Hanson Place in the Fort Greene section. Built in 1929—around the same time as the megalith Chrysler and Empire State buildings in Manhattan—and billed as "The Tower of Strength," it stretches thirty-four stories, from its handsome banking floor to the tip of its domed tower, adorned with four illuminated clocks that can be seen for miles around.

But most of Brooklyn's other "showplace" structures are closer to the ground. Among them are the original Williamsburgh Savings Bank at 175 Broadway at the foot of the Williamsburg Bridge. Designed by George B. Post and built in 1875, this florid bit of Victoriana—with fine cast-iron ornamentation inside and out—is noted for its dome set on a Roman base, a solid, serious place in which to

Previous page
The Brooklyn Museum entrance with Daniel Chester French's two female statues representing Manhattan on the left, and Brooklyn on the right. *The Brooklyn Museum, Photograph Collection*

Williamsburgh Savings Bank, the Banking Hall. *The Pennsylvania State University Libraries, Historical Collections and Labor Archives, Fay S. Lincoln Collection, University Park, Pennsylvania*

Williamsburgh Savings Bank Tower, built in 1929. *Photograph © Tony Velez*

Detail of the frieze on the Eighth Avenue side of the Montauk Club, depicting the history of the Montauk Indians. *Photograph © Jeffrey Foxx*

The Montauk Club, a Venetian Gothic palazzo, built in 1891 in Park Slope. *Photograph © Tony Velez*

keep your money. Banks, in fact, star among Brooklyn's public buildings. Even more grandiose is the earlier (1868) Kings County Savings Bank—now the American Savings Bank—also in Williamsburg at 135 Broadway, a gem of Second Empire design with a hipped roof and a lively façade of pedimented windows, columns, and bandings of rusticated stone.

Few private club buildings are left in Brooklyn today, but there was never anything like the incredible Montauk Club, still resplendent in Park Slope. Inspired by the palazzi of Venice, this true architectural treasure—designed by the prolific Francis H. Kimball and completed in 1891—has a wonderfully busy brick-and-terracotta façade that mixes American Indian and Renaissance motifs. There are loggias, balconies, and traceried Gothic windows along with a band of carved Indian heads above the entrance. These and a narrative frieze above the third-story windows celebrate the exploits of the Montauks, Indians who inhabited the eastern end of Long Island.

Luxury hotels once flourished in Brooklyn Heights, but those days are long gone. The 1889 Hotel Margaret, designed by Frank Freeman in a vigorous Romanesque Revival style and, innovatively for that date, constructed of metal and glass, once sheltered art and literary celebrities—the etcher Joseph Pennell, the novelists Sigrid Undset and Betty Smith. It was destroyed by a fire in 1980 while undergoing renovation. The Hotel Pierrepont at 55 Pierrepont Street, built in 1928 and adorned with gargoyles in the last of the old-world styles, is now a senior citizens' residence. The luxurious Towers Hotel at 25 Clark Street, opened the same year, now houses members of the Jehovah's Witnesses sect. So does the Bossert at 98

30127

Hotel St. George. *Queensborough Public Library, Long Island Division*

Preceding pages:
The swimming pool at the old Hotel St. George. *Private collection*

Montague Street, a smaller but equally elegant hotel put up in 1909 for a millwork manufacturer, Louis Bossert, and for many years a hub of Brooklyn social life. It has lost its beautiful ballroom, the yachtlike Marine Roof, but the imposing lobby, with massive columns and a coffered ceiling, has been beautifully restored by the Witnessses.

RESTORATION AND RENAISSANCE

It would be no exaggeration to say that, compared with the past, new building today occurs at a glacial pace. And that is probably all to the good. Fortunately, the emphasis now, as in other cities, is on recycling the sturdy, still highly functional buildings that have survived from the nineteenth and early twentieth centuries. A sorry exception is Cadman Plaza, an ugly urban-renewal project that went up in the 1950s and 60s, comprising a park, shops, and middle-income apartments. The project was aesthetically costly: blocks of fine old Heights houses were razed, including one where Walt Whitman set the type for *Leaves of Grass* in 1855. Since the late 1950s, a strong brownstone revival movement has been underway,

Grand Hotel

From the 1930s to the 1960s, two of Brooklyn's most heavily booked entertainment spots were the vast salt-water swimming pool and the Grand Ballroom of architect Augustus Hatfield's Hotel St. George—at 51 Clark Street. The pool, 40 by 120 feet, was fed by a series of artesian wells beneath the hotel, with water half as salty as that of the sea. The glass tiles that lined its ceiling created a dazzling montage of light and images. Johnny Weismueller, Buster Crabbe, and Eleanor Holm disported there, and so did everyone else. Directly above the pool was the Grand Ballroom, measuring 136 by 116 feet and said to be the largest of any hotel in the world. Its decor was created by Colorama, a device that produced a changing sequence of colored light and shadows by means of 12,000 bulbs.

But time and urban decay ate away at the St. George. Affected by salt-water corrosion, the tiled ceiling had caved into the pool pit, and the steel supporting columns, which held up thirty stories of hotel above them, were in serious disrepair. The decorative tiles that adorned the columns had been badly vandalized. And the ballroom was filled with rubble.

In the 1980s, however, Eastern Athletic Clubs have turned the pool and the ballroom into a handsome health facility. They've decked over most of the pool with a gymnasium floor and running track, retaining a remnant of the shallow end for bathers. And in the Grand Ballroom, where dancers—including F. Scott and Zelda Fitzgerald—once swirled to music and banqueters put away tons of creamed chicken and peas, players now stretch their legs on four squash courts and eight racquetball courts.

Massive mosaics depicting architectural landscapes, by Hippolyte Kamenka, still line the walls in the gym area, and over the pool a fine Art Deco mosaic—buried under plaster and sheet rock—was dug out, restored, and beautifully relighted. The pool itself, often described as "a real democracy with room for everybody," was retained under the gym floor. The St. George is taking steps toward regaining its past glamour.

with thousands of young professional families reclaiming long-neglected houses in the Heights, Park Slope, Cobble Hill, Carroll Gardens, Fort Greene, Bedford–Stuyvesant, and other Brooklyn areas. Not only houses, but larger buildings are being renovated for residential, commercial, and artistic uses.

In the Heights, the massive Eagle Warehouse and Storage Company, at 28 Cadman Plaza, where the long-defunct *Brooklyn Eagle* once was printed, is now luxury condominiums. Between the Brooklyn and Manhattan bridges, the ten-part Gair and Sweeney factory is being refurbished as office buildings. In Bedford–Stuyvesant, the original stone façade of an old milk-bottling plant serves as the entrance to Restoration Plaza, which includes an art gallery, a recording studio, and the Billie Holiday Theatre. In Fort Greene, the Brooklyn Academy of Music has transformed the 1904 Majestic Theater, once a legitimate theater, then a movie house, and then a church, into an arena for live performances again. And in Red Hook, the Port Authority has spent $30 million to turn the Erie Basin Marine Terminal—built in 1864—into a high-tech fishing village.

But new building projects are happening. The most spectacular of those that have reached completion is One Pierrepont Plaza in downtown Brooklyn, a nineteen-story tower that is the borough's first major commercial office building in a quarter of a century. Known as the Morgan Stanley Building for its chief tenant, the brokerage firm, the structure has a brick-and-limestone exterior designed to blend into the Heights neighborhood. Nearby is Livingston Plaza, a $65-million, twelve-story office building in masonry and glass designed by the Chicago architect Helmut Jahn. Significant to the downtown area is Brooklyn Renaissance Plaza, a thirty-story hotel-and-office complex to be built directly across from the Supreme Court Building.

These new projects indicate that the battered borough is on the rise again. Its architectural environment alone—a stock of sturdy

Empire Stores, built in 1885: a group of post–Civil War warehouses. *Photograph Berenice Abbott. Collections of the Municipal Archives of the City of New York, W.P.A. Writers' Project*

industrial buildings, hundreds of brownstones and limestones that could not be matched by today's construction practices, and first-rate public facilities—parks, beaches, and cultural institutions— look better than ever next door to overbuilt Manhattan.

Brooklyn's personality is no less evident in its buildings than in its people. In a reflective mood, longtime Brooklynite Joe Klein, a political journalist, writes: "There are times when we all find ourselves out on the street together; the street lined with the same gloriously prim brownstones throwing precisely the same shadows as they did a century ago . . . and time—decades, even a century— becomes irrelevant. The twentieth century melts into the nineteenth, and we stand quietly at our stoops (as others will in the twenty-first century) communing with the past and each other."

Eagle Warehouse residential cooperative on Old Fulton Street, originally the Eagle Warehouse and Storage Company of Brooklyn. Built in 1893, it was turned into condominiums in 1980. *Photograph © Jeffrey Foxx*

NAMING NEIGHBORHOODS

The neighborhoods of Brooklyn evoke ethnic images and accents of their twentieth-century habitués and sons-of-habitués. Neighborhood "names" seem to go with Brooklyn, and Brooklynese. They're as natural as the Arab food on Atlantic Avenue or the Russian emigrés, their babushkas fluttering in the wind, crowding the schmaltz herring shops on Brighton Beach Avenue. The environ of bodegas, pizzerias, and Irish pubs near Flatbush Avenue still gives stand-up comics an easy laugh. In the 1941 movie musical *Ziegfeld Girl*, Lana Turner played a babe named "Flatbush." America did not forget.

The memorable names of the areas in Kings County, heard in movies, on radio, and later on television, come from history. Dutch and English founders were recognized. So were their favorite towns and cities across the ocean. The bucolic countryside itself, the Revolutionary War, Indian tribes, and early patrician families all contributed to the naming of neighborhoods.

Some examples:

Going Dutch

Coney Island, settled by the Dutch, was densely populated with rabbits *(konijn)*, which led farmers on a merry chase and ultimately to a good meal.

Bushwick (*Boswijck*, or Town of the Woods) and Flatbush (*Vlache Bos*, or Wood Plain) were two of the five original Dutch towns.

The seventeenth-century Dutch settler Hans Bergen and his descendants unpacked near the sea breezes at Bergen Beach.

Dyker Heights possibly refers to Dutch dikes constructed in marshland, though there's a chance that early landowners were Dutchmen named Van Dyke.

Irishtown

Vinegar Hill, where many Irish immigrants lived who worked in the Navy Yard, commemorates a battle in Ireland against the British in 1798.

The Peace Pipe

Canarsie was where the Canarsee Indians roamed. Gowanus was named after another tribe, the Gouwane.

Ice and Water

When a titanic glacier of the Ice Age finally melted a million years ago, it left a muddled terrain of marshes and ridges, valleys and hills. Park Slope, adjacent to Prospect Park, emerged on the gentle slope of a glacial ridge for the toffs "who lived on the hill."

Bay Ridge was originally Yellow Hook, because of the clay found there. The name was changed after a yellow fever epidemic in 1853. Red Hook took its name from the color of the clay in the land that pushed into the upper bay. And, in a bay near Coney Island, Sheepshead (in the 1880s) was the popular "catch of the day" that kept fisherman prosperous.

There'll Always Be an England

Bath Beach and Brighton Beach recall a celebrated spa and seaside resort in England. At Manhattan Beach, you'll find such streets as Oxford, Dover, Amherst, Exeter, and Kensington.

Bedford, a farming community named after the duke of Bedford in the 1600s, merged with

Stuyvesant, which honored New Amsterdam's governor Peter Stuyvesant.

Fond memories of Windsor Castle produced Windsor Terrace.

America Hurrah

Clinton Hill salutes Governor De Witt Clinton and his family, the posh folks who lived on another Brooklyn hill. Carroll Gardens is named after Charles Carroll, the Maryland signer of the Declaration of Independence. But he never lived there. Fort Greene is a tribute to the Revolutionary War general Nathaniel Greene.

Connecticut businessman John Pitkin had a dream—a community that competed with New York, so he established East New York in 1835.

Egbert and Henry Benson, statesmen during the Revolutionary period, were landowners who settled Bensonhurst.

In the mid-nineteenth century real estate developer Charles S. Brown encouraged Eastern European immigrants to move to his subdivision known as Brownsville.

Crow Hill went uppity at the turn of the century with an "n" and became Crown Heights.

Rising high above the East River, Brooklyn Heights, once called Clover Hill, was one of New York's first suburbs.

The historically named hills, boulevards, slopes, districts, ridges, and beaches could be playfully re-created as a "financial" board game like Monopoly—called Brooklyn. A roll of the dice and guess what? You might buy a house in Cobble Hill where a small fort, during the American Revolution, warned that the British were coming. Today that house is part of the "Brownstone Revolution"—and Manhattanites are coming!

Lana Turner played a girl called "Flatbush" in *Ziegfeld Girl*. *Cinemafile, Inc.*

Arts and Flowers

CURTAIN UP!

Isadora Duncan, the freewheeling spirit who stripped modern dance of scenery, point shoes, and tutus, leaped barefoot across the stage of the Brooklyn Academy of Music in 1908. In her costume of diaphanous draperies, the first "star" of modern dance, whose running, jumping, and flitting movements brought to life the figures she admired on Greek vases, played to a packed house. Before the doors of the Academy had opened, tickets were sold out and a long, impatient line of carriages, with ladies in furs and gentlemen in top hats, clogged the entrance to Brooklyn's very own citadel of culture.

For the titian haired Isadora, who had started a craze of barefoot dancers on two continents and who unbound her hair to achieve complete naturalness onstage, the booking in Brooklyn was as important as her concert in Carnegie Hall across the river. For, in those days, Brooklyn conferred as much prestige as Manhattan. Brooklynites fell in love with her—seeing the same passion, motion, and independence that they cherished in themselves. Duncan's melodic abandon—her outstretched arms, her head thrown back almost out of sight, her naked feet flying high—brought raucous cheers at the opera house. There was more controversy about Isadora's bare feet than the bare bums, and more, that seven decades later is almost expected at the Brooklyn Academy of Music, which now presents avant-garde performers who never even appear in Manhattan.

"Call it a renaissance of music and drama and art," says guitarist Richie Havens, a frequent Academy performer who first began singing with his neighborhood pals on the streets of Brooklyn. "It's happening here *again*, and yeah, we're cheering."

The Brooklyn Academy of Music, known by its Pop-sounding acronym, BAM, is America's oldest center for the performing arts. It has endured fire, flood, and a twelve-hour production, *The Life and Times of Joseph Stalin*, by Robert Wilson, whose poetic theater of trance (or hypnotic repetitiveness, depending upon your artistic permissiveness) requires that audiences leave their free will at the checkroom. When the Academy opened on Montague Street in

Isadora Duncan in "La Marseillaise," 1917. *Photograph © Arnold Genthe. Museum of the City of New York*

The Opera House, Brooklyn Academy of Music. *Brooklyn Academy of Music*

1861—it burned down in 1903, and the present one opened in 1908—there was no Metropolitan Opera House in New York. In fact, across America you could count the number of opera houses on the fingers of one hand. And it remained that way for years to come. In New York, if you wanted to hear opera, you attended the Academy of Music in lower Manhattan, which opened in 1854, complete with red-and-gold boxes, where Edith Wharton and Henry James heard *Faust*. The Metropolitan, a remote distance from social Washington Square, "near the forties," lamented a horrified Mrs. Wharton, did not part its great gold curtain until almost thirty years later. So the highbrow performance arts began at the Academy of Music in Manhattan and the Brooklyn Academy of Music.

The original BAM in Brooklyn Heights presented the works of Donizetti, Puccini, and Verdi. The operas were in Italian, and, if the plots dealt with deception, thievery, murder, rape, kidnapping, madness, and other mischievous behavior, the board at BAM really did not blanch. It happened in a foreign language. It was sung. It was *bellissimo*! But one of the Academy's founders, who considered spoken drama, even if by Shakespeare, the work of the Devil, announced that there would be no production of plays. The stage was to be used only for "refined entertainment." The good citizens of Brooklyn, led by strong editorials in *The Brooklyn Eagle*, denounced this sanctimonious posturing. But after the Academy was used for a demonstration in the training of wild horses, its philistine board finally lost its clout. Some months later *Hamlet* opened a season of the classics. Tongue-in-cheek, *The Eagle* reported the Bard's arrival, stating that "should the city be overwhelmed by an earthquake anytime during the day" it would be a natural act and not a punishment from God.

The big names and companies played at the Academy. D'Oyly Carte presented *The Pirates of Penzance*, Ralph Waldo Emerson lectured on Transcendentalism, Paderewski played the piano, Fritz Kreisler the violin and, in 1896, Eleanora Duse gave one of her last coughs in *Camille*—her "first and only appearance in Brooklyn this season." The Academy had attained legendary status. But long before Duse, a lesser-known player appeared who was later to make headlines for his infamy. In 1863 he was in that tragedy of treachery *Richard II*. His name was John Wilkes Booth.

By the turn of the century, the Academy was firmly established as a symbol of civilized sociability. Unfortunately, like many playhouses of its day, it was a worrisome fire trap. Late one evening in November 1903, during preparations for a political banquet, a stray spark became a fire, and within twenty minutes the auditorium was a blazing volcano of flame. Crumbling walls crushed a saloon next

Adelina Patti's "Farewell Program," an advertisement for Creme Simon. *Brooklyn Academy of Music*

Ceiling of the Opera House, Brooklyn Academy of Music. *Brooklyn Academy of Music*

door, and other surrounding buildings caught fire. But the public-spirited Brooklynites considered the construction of a new Academy "a patriotic privilege and duty." Restored to life in an area near Brooklyn Heights—today a slightly seedy no-man's land—the prestigious architectural team of Henry B. Herts and Hugh Tallant, who designed many gemlike theaters in New York, imaginatively put together an exceptional complex, Neo-Renaissance in style—exceptional because the two-thousand-seat opera house, with a chandelier once described as a glittering Fabergé egg, has the inti-

Harvey Lichtenstein, President and Executive Producer of the Brooklyn Academy of Music, in the Lepercq Space. *Photograph © Rob Kinmonth. Brooklyn Academy of Music*

Dance Theatre Wuppertal performing "Carnation," choreographed by Pina Bausch, at the Brooklyn Academy of Music. *Brooklyn Academy of Music*

macy of a drawing room. There, tucked into the cream-colored brick edifice, are a cozy playhouse that seats around one thousand and a ballroom now used for experimental works and performance art.

The official opening in 1908 extended over several months and included a ruckus over the naked cupids in the ballroom (quickly adorned with fig leaves), a scramble for tickets to hear Madame Ernestine Schumann-Heink's only concert "in this country this season," and a traffic tie-up over the arrival of the Metropolitan Opera with its two great stars, Geraldine Farrar and Enrico Caruso. The Met, in fact, played a season at the Academy until the early 1920s. Once again, it became a house of history—the setting for Humperdinck's new opera, *Königskinder*, which required a gaggle of geese and Geraldine Farrar. But the diva's pet goose, which she called Gretchen, wandered out the stage door and the soprano refused to sing until it was caught. The management found Gretchen ambling down Fulton Street.

During the Christmas season of 1916 Sarah Bernhardt astonished audiences in three roles: Camille, Cleopatra, and Joan of Arc. She was seventy-three years old and stumping the boards with a wooden leg. Then came an incident that seems to happen only in the movies. At the performance of *L'Elisir d'Amore* in 1921, Caruso suffered a throat hemorrhage during the first act before a horrified house, spilling blood into a handkerchief. Some opera buffs cried, "Stop him...!" The curtain came down. He died some months later. "BAM is a landmark with ghosts from the past, and stars of the future," says Brooklyn-raised musician Tom Chapin, who has performed at the Academy.

With the flight of families to the suburbs after World War II, the house fell upon hard times but managed to limp along. Its rebirth started in the late 60s when Harvey Lichtenstein became director. Combining the artistic eye of Diaghilev with the business sense of Sol Hurok, the Brooklyn-born impresario (who studied dance with Merce Cunningham) put the Academy again on the international cultural circuit. When the post was offered, Lichtenstein, who had been associated with the New York City Ballet, was warned by well-meaning friends, "Don't go there. It's a situation with no possibility. It's dead." But Lichtenstein, who longed to have a theater of his very own, saw it as a big chance. Under his stewardship BAM, bursting with life, has become a thriving alternative to Broadway and Lincoln Center. The feeling at BAM is: Don't replicate what's being done in Manhattan.

"Listen, I grew up in an area called Bedford–Stuyvesant," says Lichtenstein, remarkably amiable and relaxed despite constant flights around the world, scouting theater and dance companies. "I was an only child. My father worked in a factory that made straw hats for women. We were poor but didn't do without art. I studied the violin as a kid, so I always had a real interest in music. My fantasy life was tied up in baseball and music. Toscanini—I heard him play at the Academy." A faraway smile crosses his face. "I grew up and found myself an impresario in my *hometown*. It's a crazy dream come true."

BAM gives Brooklyn a strong sense of identity, and its productions give Brooklyn a role in shaping the country's taste. When worldly visitors come to town, they always ask, "What's happening at the Academy?" Lichtenstein started the Next Wave Festival, a seasonal event that revels in risk with mixed-media events by Meredith Monk, sassy turns by choreographer Twyla Tharp and her dancers, sonic assaults by new-wave composer Glenn Branca, and meditative music by Philip Glass. Those who attend are mostly under the age of forty, often with punk hairstyles, deliberately bag-

gy suits, and slit-up-the-thigh dresses. They're closer to the crowds roaming through SoHo's art galleries on a Saturday night than the bepearled patrons gathered at the Metropolitan Opera on a Monday night. Add tap dance extravaganzas and salutes to the big band era of Lionel Hampton and Count Basie and it's easy to see why the Academy is a conversation piece at cocktail parties. A tribute to the Brooklyn-born composer George Gershwin was a startling experience for BAM's younger patrons, who suddenly realized that

The old Majestic Theatre. *New-York Historical Society*

The Majestic Theatre prior to its 1987 renovation as one of the theaters of the Brooklyn Academy of Music. *Photograph © David Epstein. Brooklyn Academy of Music*

American musical comedy ends rather than starts with the unhummable melodies of Stephen Sondheim. Manhattanites always demand a "don't miss" cultural gala at least every other season (to ask for more would be downright churlish), and to no one's surprise, it often means a round-trip to Brooklyn. In 1987, the Academy took over a decaying old theater a block and a half away called the Majestic. Defying convention, it spent $5 million to create an ambience of exposed brick walls and ducts, fragments of chipped friezes, peeling paint, and Spartan benches arranged in a sort of wraparound amphitheater setting. There's nothing comfortable about the Majestic. It's an "environmental" restoration—the old made newer, with new plumbing, wiring, lobbies, and dressing rooms—that brings an abandoned building to life. The opening production was Peter Brooks's *The Mahabharata*, a dramatized version of a Sanskrit poem written three thousand years ago, with a running time of nine hours that could not, according to Lichtenstein, be done "within the commercial theater." Lichtenstein remains a solid, unflappable force—whether he's preparing for the West German choreographer Pina Bausch, whose dancers express themselves amidst a field of fresh carnations, or confronting, as he once did, a flood, when a water main burst under the street, destroying costumes and scenery and filling up half of the opera house itself. The staff tramped around in fishing boots for two weeks, but the show eventually went on.

Summing up the impresario who gives New Yorkers an opportunity to mull new electronic collaborations between Merce Cunningham and John Cage or the rhythmic complexities of Steven Reich, the critic Clive Barnes says, "He tries something and if that doesn't work he tries something else. But always, right from the beginning he had a genuine affinity for the avant-garde. He has made BAM into one of the cultural centers of New York."

ARTFUL EYES

The Brooklyn Museum was originally founded as a kind of library to "shield young men from evil associations and . . . encourage improvement during leisure hours." The present building, constructed on the tree-lined Eastern Parkway in 1897, was Brooklyn's proud answer to the Metropolitan Museum of Art at a time when the borough was a prosperous rival. The museum today ranks seventh in the country in term of its collections. "If we were anywhere else in the country," asserts director Robert Buck, "we'd be recognized for what we are—one of the best museums in the world."

So, by the turn of the century, Brooklyn not only had its own opera house, but also its own museum—a culturally dynamic duo

Martin Puryear lobby installation, November 18, 1988–February 13, 1989, in the lobby of the Brooklyn Museum. *The Brooklyn Museum*

Section of the "Hall of the Americas" at the Brooklyn Museum. *The Brooklyn Museum*

Robert Buck, Director of the Brooklyn Museum. *Photograph Louis Goldman. The Brooklyn Museum*

Albert Bierstadt. Storm in the Rocky Mountains, Mt. Rosalie, *1866. Oil on canvas, 83 x 142½ in. The Brooklyn Museum*

that most American cities lacked. There was a period, starting after World War II, when, like BAM, the museum limped along in the shadow of its more charismatic Manhattan sisters. But, encouraged by BAM's programming, which has clearly stimulated people on both sides of the Bridge, the Brooklyn Museum decided to shake off its identity crisis. In the early 80s, it hired a creative go-getter, Robert Buck, who brings an evangelistic personality to his directorship. Former director of the Albright-Knox Art Gallery in Buffalo, Buck is spreading word of the museum with eye-popping exhibitions and ambitious plans for its building. A New Englander, Buck himself plunked his family down in a Queen Anne–style house near Brooklyn College. "I didn't want to live in Manhattan," he explains. "My instinct was to *stay where the action is.*"

The Beaux Arts structure was planned as the world's largest museum but was never completed. Buck has launched a daring multi-million-dollar campaign for expansion and renovation, which is intended to include restoring the monumental limestone staircase that pyramided from the street to the main entrance on the third floor. The steps were removed during the Depression by the Works Progress Administration. No one knows exactly why. Rumors persist of faulty construction and a feeling that Neoclassicism had simply gone out of fashion. Their dismantling, at any rate, gave plenty of work to the unemployed. "I think the idea was to bring the temple down to the people," suggests Buck, "to make it seem more accessible during hard times." On either side of the ground-level main entrance stand Daniel Chester French's statues representing Manhattan and Brooklyn, removed from the Manhattan Bridge when the ramps were widened in the early 60s. Today, according to Buck, the statue of Brooklyn also symbolizes progress.

"A Museum of Everything for Everybody" is how the museum historically describes itself. Long before the present building went up there existed in Brooklyn Heights a museum that was combined with the village post office, police court, and a library. The marquis de Lafayette laid the cornerstone on the Fourth of July, 1825, and a small boy named Walt Whitman, observing the ceremony, recalled many years later the excitement of the hour: "The day was a re-

Go West, Young Man

One of the museum's most idiosyncratic curators, R. Stewart Culin, filled the exhibition halls, the attic, and the basement with twelve thousand objects. Culin joined the staff in 1903 and traveled round the world during the next twenty-five years, usually with a staff artist who painted backdrops for exhibitions he mounted of Indian, African, and Oceanic art. He was particularly keen on finding pieces by the vanishing North American Indians. From the south- and northwest, Culin sent Indian masks, dolls, ceremonial regalia, carved sheets, gigantic totems, ladders, pottery, and doors back to the museum. He worked with traders, missionaries and, literally, went from door to door making purchases from the Indians themselves.

Stewart Culin was often away for months. Boxes would arrive from California or New Mexico, and exasperated assistants wrote him, "Please tell us what's here and *what we're to do with it?*" An obsessed person who operated on a shoestring budget, Culin forced the museum to see his "primitive" acquisitions as art. And, indeed, he got them in the nick of time. It wasn't long after his last expedition in the 1920s that the Indian "heirlooms" had all but disappeared from their villages. Culin, who came from Philadelphia, made Brooklyn his home—when he wasn't with "the Pueblo people."

Curators are quickly forgotten, but Stewart Culin's seemingly mad expeditions (he never announced in advance where he was going), his priceless and unique collection of American Indian artifacts, and his flair for showmanship (he liked to be seen in Navajo costume on horseback) have firmly established his name at the Brooklyn Museum. "Culin single-handedly steered the museum in the direction of primitive art," says Robert Buck, as he pores over archival material from a Culin exhibition. "And he was installing shows here while the various wings of the museum were still being built."

The late Stewart Culin, curator at the Brooklyn Museum, 1903–28. *The Brooklyn Museum Archives, Culin Archival Collection*

117

markably beautiful one. The boys and girls of Brooklyn were marshalled at the old ferry in two lines . . . with a wide space between them. Lafayette came over in a carriage from New York, passed slowly through the lines. The whole thing was old-fashioned, quiet, natural." Whitman lived to see the building become the Brooklyn Institute on Washington Street, minus the post office and court, where lectures, readings, courses in drawing, and an art gallery made it the intellectual hub of Brooklyn. But that building was destroyed by fire in 1890, shortly before Whitman's death, and Brooklynites proceeded to raise money for the massive museum on the Parkway that now holds about two million art objects. The Brooklyn Museum was dedicated to welcoming "the tired mechanic or laboring man or domestic . . . who comes to gain a little knowledge that is elsewhere inaccessible to him of the secrets of nature or the triumphs of art."

And here secrets from the past and unexpected triumphs are revealed. The rich Egyptian collection includes an ointment spoon in the shape of a poppy, which may have come from the Tutankhamen tomb. There are Chinese bronzes inlaid with silver from the late Chou period, costumes from nineteenth-century Japan, and sculptured wooden dolls from what was once called the Belgian Congo. Put in any other city, the museum's pre-Colombian, Egyptian, and decorative works would make scholars, critics, and collectors purr with delight and envy. It also has splendid nineteenth- and twentieth-century art. Visitors are haunted by the power of Albert Bierstadt's *Storm in the Rocky Mountains, Mt. Rosalie* (1866) and the chilling beauty of George Bellows's *A Morning Snow—Hudson River* (1910). Other masterworks in the collection are by artists Winslow Homer, Gilbert Stuart, Thomas Eakins, and John Singer Sargent. But one of the prizes is by Francis Guy, who left England in 1795 and sailed to America, where he lived in Brooklyn for almost twenty years. His *Winter Scene in Brooklyn*, painted from his window on Front Street around 1820 or so, captures a town aglow with energy as his neighbors saw logs, feed chickens, run errands, water horses, or just stand around and chat—a favorite Brooklyn activity, continued over the years on porches, fire escapes, rooftops, and at the candy store on the corner.

The diversity of the museum mirrors Brooklyn's population. White marble nymphs, plaster casts of Greek sculpture such as the *Discus Thrower* and *Winged Victory*, and a Chinese cloisonné doghouse—they're all there, or somewhere in storage. Meanwhile, Buck is installing shows while dramatically altering the Grand Lobby and using it as a gallery for his own passionate interest in contemporary art, the direction in which he's pushing the museum. Many of the works he shows can't be seen in Manhattan. He presented the imposing wooden sculpture of Martin Puryear, whose objects convey the sensation of heroic movement, and also exhibited the controversial, Brooklyn-born Robert Longo, whose three-dimensional works of love, death, and power make him one of the livelier presences on the scene.

"We're not on Fifth Avenue," adds Buck. "We can't put on the big line-'em-up 'blockbuster' shows. We're not on the tourist beat. But we're attracting the young who are moving here again and senior citizens, and a special art crowd from Manhattan that knows we offer something different." Under Buck, museum attendance has climbed and, at openings, there's always a line of limos that have crossed the Bridge. "Since the Bridge was built, it has consistently fed the mainstream of Manhattan. Now I believe the reverse will happen. We'll be seeing great changes all over Brooklyn by the end of *this* century. It will have come, in its own extraordinary way, full circle."

BORDERS, BEDS, SHRUBBERIES

An oasis of serenity in New York? Where time is absent and you can almost hear the silence? Where there are flower beds, ponds, and trees and no one to disturb your meditations? And, it's all free? Sounds impossible, but such a Shangri-la exists in Brooklyn, tucked away behind the Brooklyn Museum on Washington Avenue. The serene Botanic Garden captures the changing seasons—the explosion of pink in spring, the burst of yellow in summer, the burnished browns of autumn, and the raw limbs of winter. It was founded in 1910 on a city dump, where bonfires burned, and became an "urban miracle," a mixture of science and beauty that extends over 50 acres. With its four thousand rosebushes of seven hundred varieties, along with Japanese cherry trees, lilacs, tulips, crabapples, azaleas, wisterias, and water lilies—to name a few of the fifteen thousand plants and flowers—the Botanic Garden, like BAM and the Brooklyn Museum, has an international reputation. It draws about seven hundred fifty thousand visitors from around the world each year.

No radios are allowed. No graffiti. No bicycles or skateboards. No munchies or beverages. No jogging or exercising of pets. The Garden, where you can meander among the evergreen, cedar, and spruce trees for hours or sit on a bench (but not on the lawn, except in the Cherry Esplanade) is a kind of living museum itself. The botanists experiment in plant breeding and even have plant patients. The first all-yellow magnolia, called the Elizabeth, was created here and presented to the queen of England's gardener at

The Steinhardt Conservatory, which houses a Tropical Pavilion and a Desert Pavilion. Its prize exhibit, however, is the collection of bonsai unequaled in the Americas. *The Brooklyn Botanic Garden*

Under a Willow Tree

The novelist Gerald Green, who grew up in Brooklyn, where his father was a doctor and inspiration for his best-seller *The Last Angry Man*, once reminisced, "Luckily, the opportunity to enjoy trees and flowers, lawns and gardens is still one of the great boons that Brooklyn has to offer. I refer, of course, to the Brooklyn Botanic Garden, that island of peace and beauty in the heart of my favorite borough. I can remember as a boy of eleven, accompanied by my cousin, trudging off on a 'hike' to the Garden, there to rest in the shade of a willow tree. I have no idea what we discussed as we stared at the sky. But it was great fun—even though we took a ribbing from local

roughs who sneered at our stroll in the sylvan glades. I remember with pleasure the Japanese Garden, a miracle of grace, style and harmony, and the greenhouses, and the thoughtfully labeled shrubs and trees. The wisest man I ever knew, the naturalist and philosopher Joseph Wood Krutch, once said that he would like best to be remembered as 'An Inspector of Wildflowers.' It is not a bad way to spend one's leisure time. As Krutch once said, *God looked at the world and found that it was good—and how nice to be able to agree with Him from time to time!* In the Brooklyn Botanic Garden, this condition is always apparent, palpable and there for the eye to delight in."

Windsor Castle. The many gardens-within-the-Garden include herb and rock beds, a fragrance area for the blind, and the Shakespeare Garden where eighty plants, herbs, and spices mentioned by the Bard abound in gleeful display. A popular spot, especially for weddings, is the Japanese Garden, elegantly spread over an acre and designed in 1914 by the Japanese architect Takeo Shiota. Cascades of water flow over rocks into a storybook pond crossed by bridges to a tea house surrounded by evergreens and cherry and wisteria blossoms. With its greenhouse, the Garden boasts on the coldest day of the year, "You can get to a tropical rain forest for the price of a subway token."

The Desert Pavilion in the Brooklyn Botanic Garden. *Photograph © John Calabrese. The Brooklyn Botanic Garden*

Red, Hot, and Blues

...this is my story...
...this is my song...
praising the Saviour,
all the day long...

Eight singer-actors are clustered around the orchestra pit at the Billie Holiday Theatre in the heart of Bedford–Stuyvesant, a neighborhood of weedy lots, restored and burnt-out brownstones, shops and markets, the aimless wanderers and those whose focus is to make Bed–Stuy a strong middle-class community despite "inner-city" problems. The theater at 1368 Fulton Street devotes itself to black plays, written and directed by black artists, and aimed at black audiences. Operating since 1972, the nonprofit theater, started on federal grants, is a pivotal force in the redevelopment of Bedford–Stuyvesant. It has not only proved an inspirational source to the community but has become known for its vivid productions examining the black experience in American life, drawing audiences from Cleveland, Detroit, Toledo, and Atlanta. It's called, affectionately, "The Billie."

The performers gathered at the piano are doing a brush-up musical rehearsal after a Sunday matinee of The Billie's long-run hit *Blues for a Gospel Queen*, a biography of Mahalia Jackson. The show combines original songs with gospel hymns Mahalia Jackson learned as a child and later made famous. And the thirty-member cast belts out each number with boundless enthusiasm and a kind of religious razzmatazz.

> *This little light of mine...*
> *I'm going to make it shine...*
> *Make it shine...*

During the rehearsal, Maurice Carlton, who plays Mahalia's scamp of a first husband, explains, "I lived with my wife and kids in Manhattan but moved to Brooklyn just to be near The Billie. People complain that Broadway doesn't do black theater. Well this—" he gestures around the intimate jewel box house—218 plush seats, exposed brick walls—"is ours, there's a richness here you wouldn't find on Broadway." Then he laughs, "You'd never guess this was once a milk bottling factory." Carlton, a striking man in his thirties, comes from Michigan, where he studied acting, and was an original member of The Billie. He worked in a Manhattan advertising agency and now sells real estate, but, he explains, "This is my real job. I love it here. To give six performances a week, and sell houses, too, I take a lot of vitamins." Before returning to the musical rehearsal, Carlton adds, "The theater, *our theater*, gives us time to stop and see what's beautiful about ourselves."

The bouyant company, which always impresses visitors—Sam Goldwyn, Jr., casting directors from The Public Theater and *Miami Vice*, the curious from Manhattan—has won playwrights Samm-Art Williams *(Home)* and Charles Gordone *(No Place to Be Somebody)* honor and Pulitzer prizes. A young dancer named Debbie Allen, who got her start at The Billie, starred in a revival of *Sweet Charity*. Marjorie Moon, The Billie's producer, says, "Equally important is what it does for audiences. Many have never been in a theater before. They can't afford the $50 price on Broadway." At The Billie, tickets range from $6 to $12, and there's a discount for groups, who arrive in buses specially chartered for showtime in Bed–Stuy. When Marjorie Moon began producing, she discovered that the neighborhood had such a negative image that some were afraid to attend. "So I made the rounds of churches, telling the ministers, 'We're in the same business—spiritual enrichment.' Gradually we

Exploring the natural world at the Brooklyn Children's Museum, c. 1900 (this page) and today (opposite). *The Brooklyn Children's Museum*

developed a devoted audience. We helped give Bed–Stuy a *positive* image." She proudly shows a mailing list of five hundred schools, clubs, and churches that are always eager to book the next attraction at The Billie.

The Billie isn't just song and dance. With a modest $400,000 yearly budget, it strives to provoke and stimulate "and make people think hopefully," adds Marjorie Moon. After the Mahalia Jackson musical, she scored again with three new plays by black women about "the pain of reunion and joy of spiritual renewal."

"Spirit" is a word Marjorie Moon uses often. Spirit is what The Billie has plenty of—Spirit and esprit.

Enchanted Land

First lodged in two Victorian mansions, The Brooklyn Children's Museum was the first of its kind in the world when it opened in 1899. The farsighted founders believed that the offspring of Brooklynites should have an education complementary to the schools, concentrating on science and invention. The museum, now located

in a modern domed building at 145 Brooklyn Avenue, has a collection of forty thousand artifacts.

A ripple tank demonstrates sound waves. A windmill shows the link between energy and power. A model of a human ear explains how we often hear what we don't want to listen to. A nineteenth-century steam engine, with fly wheel, oil cup, steam vent, and whistle, nostalgically recalls steam energy. A stream that splashes through a neon-lit tunnel demonstrates, with waterwheels and gates, how water power can be harnessed. A mountainous molecular maze of space-age plastic beckons climbers and crawlers. In cabinets covered with glass are lizards and hermit crabs. There are plants, minerals, fossils, rocks, a 14-foot python, a human skeleton, and a spongy old thing that just happens to be a human brain.

The Brooklyn Children's Museum has become a model for more than two hundred similar museums around the world, from Japan to Scotland. Whatever the language, whatever the country, when the question is asked, "Where'd you get the idea?" the answer is always, "Brooklyn."

Trees of Knowledge

___

REPORT CARDS

Brooklyn is also the borough of the schoolhouse—the little red brick schoolhouse, the big white Colonial one, Victorian castles, those with Gothic gates and Tiffany windows, and, of course, the ubiquitous glass boxes that seem to attract bullet holes—or perhaps just shots from a BB gun.

Brooklyn College ranks among the best liberal arts schools in the country. Brooklyn Polytechnic rivals Princeton and Carnegie-Mellon in the field of electrophysics. The Pratt Institute is world famous for its courses in art, design, and fashion. Business, medicine, law, the performing arts, foreign languages, animal care, aviation, mechanics—there's a school for just about any field in Brooklyn.

Altogether, 60,000 undergraduates work toward degrees in eleven colleges. There are almost 800 secondary public and private schools attended by 425,000 students whose young graduates have achieved all kinds of fame: the mentally muscular Bobby Fischer, who won the United States chess championship five times (the first in 1958 when he was only fourteen) attended Erasmus Hall in Flatbush, and the physically powerful Sandy Koufax, that amazing Dodgers pitcher, went to Lafayette High School in Bensonhurst.

Brooklyn has had its ups and downs in the quality of education and school facilities, but the borough is again taking steps to see that scholarship is high. The tacitly agreed-upon game, "Go to the head of your class," whether you favor mathematics or the media, is the educational priority.

Given Brooklyn's history, it's no surprise that the nation's first free school was started by the Reformed Dutch Church in 1661 at Fulton and Bridge streets. Education flourished with hopes that theological seminaries would soon be established. That didn't happen, but there are today plenty of religious schools. Twelve Catholic high schools attract 47,000 teenagers; for orthodox Jews, there are 129 yeshivas and day schools; and St. Francis College in Brooklyn Heights, founded in 1884 by the Franciscans, has 2,000 students devoted to both spiritual and intellectual attainments. In the

Erasmus Hall Museum (originally, Erasmus Hall Academy), built in 1786, in the courtyard of Erasmus Hall High School. *Photograph © Tony Velez*

Quaker tradition, the Brooklyn Friends School in downtown Brooklyn has 360 students. There's something for everyone. In fact, private schools and colleges lure students from the other four boroughs and New Jersey.

CAP AND GOWN

Actually, students first started coming to Brooklyn from near and far when the historic Erasmus Hall Academy (later High School) opened in Flatbush in September 1787, a few days after the signing of the Constitution. It had a number of boarding pupils from other states, and many students from Manhattan lived during the week with well-to-do Dutch farmers who proudly hosted young scholars pursuing Milton's *Paradise Lost* and Goldsmith's *Roman History*. Named after the Dutch scholar Desidirius Erasmus, the academy was financed by notable figures of the post-Revolution days, like Alexander Hamilton and John Jay, who, with influential Brooklynites, had a craving for knowledge. Erasmus originated the grade-adviser system and had the first school library in America. As the school expanded in the twentieth century, its chapel, Gothic towers, and leafy courtyard were home for novelist Bernard Mala-

The music department didn't appreciate a student named Streisand, seen here with Elliott Gould (left) and Jack Kruschen in the Broadway show *I Can Get It for You Wholesale*, 1962. *UPI/Bettmann*

mud, publisher Earl Graves of *Black Enterprise Magazine*, and the basketball coach Billy Cunningham.

By the 1980s, the once elite Erasmus—long part of the public school system—had stumbled on hard times. It had a dropout rate and attendance record among the worst in New York. The school's broken windows, trash-strewn halls, and leaking ceilings led the faculty and students to feel abandoned by the Board of Education. But, just before Erasmus celebrated its two-hundredth birthday, it received a coat of fresh paint from top to bottom, an infusion of money from the Board of Education, and along with both, a sense of fresh energy and optimism. There is hope that the golden age of Erasmus has not disappeared. At its anniversary celebration State Education Commissioner Thomas Sobol said the school's message to the city and its students was loud and clear: "Young man, young woman, you are not allowed to grow up ignorant. *This society needs you.*"

Another high school once known for its academic excellence is also struggling to make a comeback. Thomas Jefferson High, at 400 Pennsylvania Avenue, known as "Jeff," or "T.J.," where Danny

An "A" Student

"In high school, she spelled her name Barbara. She was quiet. She didn't interact with others in her class. She was more of a loner, shy and introverted. But she got top grades and graduated in 1959 with a 93 average." That's how Marilyn Sapoch sums up a student at Erasmus Hall High School, the singer with the limpid teardrop voice—Barbra Streisand. "I remember her vividly, I wonder if she remembers me," adds Sapoch, who taught science and psychology for thirty years at Erasmus.

"I know she came from a poor family. No fancy blouses and cashmeres for her. So she deliberately dressed different from everybody else. Sandals. Outlandish getups. Blue paint around her eyelids. And, oh my, the red dyes in her hair! She was in my biology class with about thirty-five others and did commendable work. I heard that she waited tables part-time in a Chinese restaurant. But she wanted to sing and learned by listening to big names on the radio. I understand today that the chairman of the music department really didn't recognize her talent. She'd sing a song *her* way, not his—and this would bother him. She was a real nonconformist, and, you know, a lot of teachers didn't like that."

A proud Brooklynite herself, Marilyn Sapoch attended Thomas Jefferson High School, Brooklyn College, and Long Island University. She has seen the demography of the school system change, with an increase in blacks, Hispanics, and Orientals, and she also remembers when nearly half of an Erasmus graduating class scored in the 90s. But adds Sapoch, "We're still trying to inspire the students, to make them hungry for more knowledge."

Reflecting on Streisand's musical gifts, which shot her to stardom three years after graduation, Barbra's former teacher asks: "I wonder if she ever thinks about Brooklyn, or has been back? We've gone through so many changes. I hear we're getting stylish now. I think she'd be quite surprised."

Kaye and Shelley Winters went to school, spent more than a half-million dollars in 1986 trying to improve a milieu fraught with tension. The school's elegant mahogany doors, vandalized and burned, were replaced with locked metal doors. The wearing of gold chains and rings, which resulted in students being robbed or beaten, was banned, and the crime rate within the school dropped. To encourage students, and thereby reverse the dropout rate at troubled schools, such as "T.J.," at least three banks—Chase Manhattan, Citibank, and the Manufacturers Hanover Trust Company—have agreed to hire a certain number of students a year who earn high school diplomas. East Brooklyn Churches, an organized community group, is pushing for greater board participation in the schools to reduce the number of dropouts.

For teenagers and younger, attending public school in Brooklyn is far from idyllic. Brazen toughs who belong to gangs menace both

He Who Got Socked

Woody Allen hated school. America's favorite nebbish, with a teasing wit and penetrating insight into the anxieties of contemporary life, admits that he only attended school sporadically. "To this day I wake up in the morning and clutch onto my bed and thank God that I don't have to go to school," once confessed the filmmaker who grew up in the Flatbush–Midwood sections of Brooklyn. Small, shy, socially insecure, he was the myopic tot in grade school—"the sockee."

The big boys, the bullies, were "the sockers." Indeed, he has undergone psychiatric analysis, in part, to deal with a fear of "getting beaten up by boys of all races and creeds." He once did a monologue about a guy named Floyd: "He used to sit in the Dumb Row at school . . . a vegetable mentality in a leather jacket." Floyd confronts the young Woody, bellowing, "Hey, Red!"

"If you want me, call me by my right name—Master . . . Heywood . . . Allen." After a pause the comedian would quickly add, "I spent that winter in a wheelchair."

Allen graduated from Midwood High School in 1953. "I have that terrible memory of reading *Silas Marner*. The only thing that made it bearable was its size. It was really tiny. I can't read a book if it's thick or has little print or starts slowly or has no immediate reward." Needling an interviewer years ago, he once said his favorite book was *Advanced Sexual Positions: How to Achieve Them Without Laughing*. Turning serious, he then admitted to admiring Kafka's "intellectual acumen," Stendahl's "brilliant structure," and George S. Kaufman, "the *only* funny American playwright."

He started writing gags as a lark in high school at age fifteen and began selling them to such columnists as Leonard Lyons and Earl Wilson. When a public relations firm asked Wilson who Allen was, he replied, "Some guy in Brooklyn." The company asked Woody if he'd write witticisms for its clients, so they'd sound smart and sassy in print. He got the job: $25 a week. He wrote most of the jokes on the subway. Freed from the shackles of high school, he met with instant success as a comedy writer for Sid Caesar and Art Carney.

Found among *Earl's Pearls*, by Master Heywood Allen, of course: "A hangover is when you don't want to come out of your room because you think your head won't fit through the door."

Master Heywood Allen honed his humor on the subway. *UPI/Bettmann*

black and white youngsters near schools. They harass and beat up students in packs of five or ten on one. In school yards and restrooms racial slurs get tossed around and so do victims of bullies. Kike, nigger, Jew-boy, black bastard, wop, spic, and fairy-faggot (for the small and sensitive) are epithets that, repeated enough, can be as crushing as body blows. Home and the neighborhood candy store are safe ground. But, at school, many are psychologically terrorized. Four new schools in Flatbush and Crown Heights may help make the going more pleasurable. For a while, the Board of Education considered giving up on some schools and closing them down. Incidents such as youngsters on the rampage, throwing bottles and debris, amid the fire of gunshots and attacks on teachers, brought to life the phrase "the blackboard jungle." But parents combined with church leaders and brave teachers to ease tensions. Now many high schools emphasize specific training, which usually isn't available to students in other cities: Clara Barton High School focuses on health; Edward R. Murrow on communications; Samuel J. Tilden on law and politics; and Midwood, the campus high school of Brooklyn College, concentrates on the liberal arts.

PRIVATE STUDIES

Recollections of Brooklyn's history are not confined to its public schools. The stolid old meets the new within the halls of the Packer Collegiate Institute at 170 Joralemon Street in Brooklyn Heights (first through twelfth grades), which was started as a girls' school in 1845 and immediately plunged into social issues by helping to raise money for the Union during the Civil War. Packer went co-educational in the early 1970s, and it now accepts the prekindergarten set for a daub of erudition without a pacifier. It has an enrollment of around seven hundred. To graduate, students must earn thirty hours of school service, usually as tutors, and thirty hours of community service, usually by spending time in hospitals, nursing homes, and day-care centers. Beyond teaching students how to get along in the world, Packer's philosophy is to prepare them for critical thinking *in* the world.

Perhaps the private school with the most rapid growth is St. Ann's School, also in the Heights (at 129 Pierrepont Street), which got underway in 1965 in the basement of St. Ann's Episcopal Church and then moved into the 1906 Crescent Athletic Club. The nonsectarian school for gifted children now has about 860 enrolled who come by bus from other boroughs and states, all of whom are precocious enough to enjoy hard work without conventional restrictions: no dress code, no student government, no grades, and no football team. The teachers themselves—specialists, enthusiasts in their

field—may be called by their first or last names, wear jacket-and-tie or jeans.

St. Ann's costs around $8,000 a year but strives to maintain a racial and social balance with scholarships. The first graduate to become a lawyer was a black woman named Heather Williams who went to Harvard University and Harvard Law School and now works for the attorney general of New York State. St. Ann's seniors are accepted wherever they apply, it seems, but in recent years the favorite schools have been Brown, Vassar, and the University of Chicago, along with Harvard, Oberlin, Bard, and Amherst tied.

St. Ann's headmaster from the beginning was and still is Stanley Bosworth. In his mind and that of his faculty, the model progressive school doesn't "fit" into any mold and neither do the students, who move along according to their talents. Some third graders are learning Chinese, others are writing sonnets or working computers. St. Ann's believes that if you can't read well, you can't survive in the world; its students perceive that reading is an amusement park in which the thrills are Aristophanes, Darwin, and Baudelaire. "They know that modern history begins in the thirteenth century in Italy," says Bosworth, "instead of when the Beatles arrived."

A calisthenics class at Packer Collegiate Institute in 1911. *Packer Collegiate Institute, Brooklyn*

Historically, Brooklyn neighborhoods are famous for their corner candy stores. St. Ann's has a candy store, but you won't find bubble gum, lollipops, or chocolate bars. There's a choice of health food, candies, fruit, or unsweetened juice. The candy store, and St. Ann's, isn't for everybody. But it's probably one of the most stimulating prep schools in the country, and it's quite "fitting" that it happens to be in Brooklyn.

GROVES OF ACADEME

Indeed, the borough is full of educational surprises. Who'd ever guess that St. Francis College in Brooklyn Heights offers a baccalaureate degree in aviation administration? With skies becoming as crowded as highways, this degree teaches technical and managerial skills in air traffic, supervising space programs, and conducting flight training. And since the college is near three of the world's busiest airports, students get to hear lectures by industry experts and later pursue jobs with top aviation employers. Polytechnic University, in a converted razor factory at 333 Jay Street in downtown Brooklyn, "scrappy and determined to be the best," was awarded a $3.2 million research grant to develop technology for the "Star Wars" project. There are three hundred engineering schools in the country, but Polytech has the second-largest enrollment. It has

In 1890 a new building at 85 Livingston Street was built for Polytechnic Institute of Brooklyn. Founded in 1854, Polytechnic moved into new quarters at 333 Jay Street in 1958 and became Polytechnic University. *Polytechnic University, Brooklyn*

Overleaf
Pratt Institute Library. *Pratt Institute, Brooklyn*

been a research center in the development of microwave physics, radar, polymers, and solving re-entry problems of the manned space vehicles.

The arts aren't neglected either. Pratt Institute in the Clinton Hill section is a hub for architecture, art, graphics, industrial design, and engineering studies. In the 1960s, when the elegant neighborhood of mansions and brownstones turned gritty and threatening after riots and Vietnam War protests, the school refused to budge from its campus and move to greener pastures. By staying put, Pratt Institute stabilized the community and today has about four thousand students in a racially mixed area. In 1887, Pratt was one of the first schools to explore "technical" education, and it influenced the others that followed. Its faculty draws upon the best designers and architects in New York. Design graduates have introduced the American public to Cuisinart, the Trim-Line phone, the IBM keyboard, the Pro-Max dryer, and aviator-shaped glasses.

The Brooklyn campus of Long Island University on Flatbush Avenue in downtown Brooklyn attracts students from seventy countries and has an intimate student-faculty ratio, with about twenty-two students in each class. It stresses humanities and com-

munication arts, social and natural sciences, and mathematics. More accountants in Brooklyn have graduated from its School of Business than from any other college. It also offers one of the top psychology programs in the New York area.

The patrician Edith Wharton of New York and Newport and European capitals would be delighted to learn that the campus is headquarters for the Edith Wharton Society. It was organized by Annette Zilversmit, professor of American and English Literature at the Brooklyn campus. A scholarly international group, the society publishes a newsletter and holds Whartonesque discussions. "More than any other writer, Edith Wharton ironically uses New York scenes and society, even neighborhoods, as metaphors for success and how we reach for it," explains Zilversmit.

GOLDEN DAYS

Brooklyn College was started in 1930—without a campus. It was located in five different downtown buildings on Pearl, Court, and Joralemon streets. For students, getting from history to science in widely separated places was a hazardous rush amidst clanging trolley cars and honking traffic. But they were made of sturdy stuff and survived, with happy memories. Attended mostly by the bright children of working-class immigrants, it soon became known as "the poor man's Harvard." And it racked up, in short order, some two hundred and fifty alumni who are presidents, vice presidents, or chairmen of corporation boards. *Who's Who in America* lists five hundred alumni and *Who's Who of American Women* has one hundred and fifty alumnae. The names include film director Paul Mazursky ('51); former congresswomen Shirley Chisholm ('46) and Barbara Boxer ('62), constitutional law expert and Harvard law professor Alan Dershowitz ('59); and the highest-ranking woman official of the American Stock Exchange, Delia McQuade Emmons ('73). The National Endowment for the Humanities, in 1984, called it "one of the few bright spots" in higher education. And two years later, *Time* cited it as one of the nine outstanding small colleges in the nation. Each year over three hundred graduates seeking careers in law are accepted at such schools as Harvard, Yale, Stanford, and the University of Pennsylvania. During the 1980s nearly all of its pre-med students were admitted to medical schools. The college's faculty has had such impressive names as violinist Itzhak Perlman, the artist Philip Pearlstein, Oscar-winning actor F. Murray Abraham, the poet Allen Ginsberg, and computer theorist Rohit Parikh. The French director Marcel Ophuls has also been a visiting professor of film. At Brooklyn College, the kid from Bed–Stuy or Crown Heights speaks the same intellectual language, from Homer to

The tower of Pratt Institute's main building. *Pratt Institute, Brooklyn*

Long Island University. The identifying symbol of the Brooklyn campus is its five-story sculpture, informally dubbed "the arch." *Photograph © Sally Mueller. Long Island University, Brooklyn*

Descartes, as the student at the Iviest of schools. Whatever your goal, says Brooklyn College, whatever your dreams, we'll help you get there. The low tuition for New Yorkers makes an ambitious future possible.

One of nine senior colleges of the City University of New York, Brooklyn College had problems in the late 1960s and lost public confidence when an open-admissions policy crowded the school with 35,000 students. A decade later, as New York City neared bankruptcy, it agreed to state demands that the college become more selective as one condition for financial rescue. Today Brooklyn College has an enrollment of 16,000 and, to get in, high school seniors must have an 80 average or rank in the top third of their class.

The magnetic force who guided the college's "rebirth" is Robert L. Hess, who became the sixth president in 1979. "When I arrived, Brooklyn College had a terrible image," recalls Hess, who lived in Brooklyn as a child and attended kindergarten a few blocks away. "The faculty was demoralized, the campus had deteriorated to a weedy state, racial tensions were strong—its future was of concern. Could the college be turned around? Students respond to a setting, so I quickly restored the lawns and plantings, and painted buildings to get rid of the decaying look. The message was 'The College Cares.'"

From his executive window he indicates a grassy, tree-lined quadrangle flanked by immaculate Georgian-style buildings—the campus that went up on a golf course, after using temporary offices in downtown Brooklyn, in 1937. The grounds are lovely today. You could be in New England or somewhere in Virginia. The restoration even affected the neighborhood beyond as home owners and small businesses felt compelled to obliterate urban squalor.

"With a return to selective admissions," Hess continues, "the faculty, which has Ivy credentials, rediscovered what it meant to teach. Our location brings us top-notch professors who want to live in New York; they don't want to rusticate in Podunk. Finally, and most importantly, I changed the curriculum, putting the excesses of the 60s behind. I want students to leave here knowing they've been *educated*." Ten required courses, including art, literature, science, mathematical reasoning, computer programming, and Western civilization and non-Western cultures, are key to the college's elevated status.

In the mid-80s, the college collected $12.5 million in a fund-raising campaign. By 1991 it had an endowment of $9.6 million. Hess, who traveled around the country establishing alumni associations, has found graduates in countries as distant as Israel and

Robert L. Hess, president of Brooklyn College. *Photograph © J. T. Miller.*
Brooklyn College

Taiwan. Among the students today are a Chinese girl born in Brazil and a Korean youth born in Paraguay. "Any school can admit minorities," Hess observes, "the trick is to get them to *succeed*."

Hess, a graduate of Yale who came to Brooklyn from the University of Illinois at Chicago, revels in presiding over one of the nation's most ethnically mixed schools. "During the 20s, Kings County had the highest number of immigrants. Parents said, 'This is America. We'll make it through hard work and our children will make it through education.' The same is true today. Students here—white, black, Hispanic, Oriental—come from the lower middle class—they're intelligent and competitive, they know they have to make it through their own efforts. There's no rich daddy to provide for them. The college is a microcosm of what Brooklyn is today: a renewal of old America with *new* immigrants."

Brooklyn College. *Photograph © Ted Beck*

BROOKLYNESE:
AN ACCENTED BOUILLABAISSE

"Ow, eez ye—ooa san?"
Brooklynese? No. That's Cockney for "Is he your son," and it's from Bernard Shaw's Cinderella comedy *Pygmalion* (which became the musical *My Fair Lady*). In this classic theater piece, Henry Higgins, a professor of phonetics, teaches a Cockney flower-seller named Eliza Doolittle how to accent her English properly and "transforms" her into a lady. In England, where accents give status or stigma, Shaw—striking a blow for social equality—sought to prove that a waif found in the muck of Covent Garden could win acceptance—if she spoke without a dialect.

Americans have never been concerned with how they sound because most regional accents—the Yankee twang, Southern drawl, Midwestern flatness—don't necessarily reveal education, financial background, or strata in society. The one uncompromising accent, however, that's legendary for its down-to-earth gutsiness and—as represented in old movies—raw good-guyism encompasses only 70.2 square miles. Known throughout the world, it's called "Brooklynese."

This distinctive *sound* pinpoints residents of Kings County where pearls and girls can be heard as *poils and goils* (which an American Professor Higgins would be straining to correct if he lived in Brooklyn and Eliza sold pressed flowers and grapevine wreaths in a floral boutique). Many celebrities from the borough blotted out Brooklynese on their own or with the help of an 'enry 'iggins. Beverly Sills has recalled, "Although my accent has always remained New York, I did at least manage to get rid of a good bit of the Brooklyn tinge. You just don't perform Gilbert and Sullivan sounding as though you came from the Ebbets Field bleachers." When Susan Hayward moved from Flatbush to Hollywood, a studio elocution coach forced her to lower her voice and emit a slow, deep sound that came from the diaphragm, not the throat. Acquiring a new tone, timbre, and modulation took months of hard work, but she remade her voice and accent—and became a star. It wouldn't have happened otherwise and she knew it.

What then *is* "Brooklynese" and how did it happen?

Brooklyn's own phonetics expert, born in the borough and raised in Bath Beach and Bensonhurst, has most of the answers. Margaret Mannix Flynn, a counselor and lecturer for the Department of Speech at Brooklyn College, explains that the origins are historic: the first muttered words came from the Canarsee Indians. Then, early Dutch settlers had to learn English quickly after New Amsterdam and Breukelen were captured by the English in 1664. (The Dutch couldn't buy a cow or a plow without speaking English, and there weren't any schoolteachers to polish up their consonants.) Following the American Revolution, New Englanders—looking for better farmland—moved to Brooklyn, bringing along their broad *a*'s: *father* emerged as *fatha*. With the Irish immigration in the nineteenth century an archaic Irish–English went into the bubbling broth. "After England conquered Ireland in the seventeenth century," says Flynn, "Ireland was removed from contact with the outside world." The Irish had difficulty with *th* and only sounded the *t*. The word *think*, for example, became the word *tink*. They also substituted an *i* sound for *oi* in the middle of a word, so that *lawyer* sounded like *liar*.

German immigrants, passing from Ellis Island to Brooklyn, and speaking English for the first time, had trouble with the *w*'s and out came a *v*: "*Vhere* is Brooklyn?" An influx of Scandinavians, whose *y*'s carried a *j* sound, added their singsong rhythm to the multinational linguistic stew. In the late nineteenth century, Jews—from Middle and Eastern Europe, who spoke Yiddish—added another musicality that turned declarative sentences into questions. ("I went to the butcher?") And the always pesky *th* acquired an *s* and *z*: "I *sink zis*" instead of "I think this." The German–Yiddish accent carries a hard *g*: "The elevator is going-*ggup*." Meantime, Czechs and Hun-

Gene Kelly and Jean Hagen in *Singin' in the Rain*. The coming of the "talkies" revealed the tough Brooklynese of a heretofore "silent" star. *Cinemafile, Inc.*

garians slipped in a *k*: "The elevator is going-*kkup*." The Italians contributed an operatic elongation. Whereas Eastern Europeans took *bank* and squeezed it into *benk*, the Italians stretched it into *bayhyank*.

"From 1900 through the 1920s, another migration arrived in Brooklyn," observes Flynn, "but unlike the other groups, they didn't come from another country. These people came from the South. When the Southern blacks arrived, they spoke a dialect. There was a good reason for this. Both the Southern blacks and the Irish came from isolated communities kept from the mainstream of society." They too had trouble with the *th*, substituting a *t* or *d*: *tat* or *dat* for that. And *ng*'s were dropped. Going became *goin'*.

In recent years Brooklyn has welcomed the tired and poor from Puerto Rico, who find an *e* sound where there should be an *i*: *ship* becomes *sheep*. Immigrants from the British West Indies speak English, continues Flynn, "with a very strong intonation pattern where the stress tends to be placed toward the end of a word. Their speech pattern is also affected by the fact that they were originally colonized by England." Newly arrived Asians grapple with *w*'s and *i*'s: *pool* sounds like *poow* and *praise* tickles the ear as *pwaise*.

In sum, the bouillabaisse of accents that produces Brooklynese reflects about two dozen languages and dialects.

"Very few places have the cultural diversity of Brooklyn," observes Flynn. "We don't tell students that it's wrong to talk Brooklynese, but for those who want to change their pronunciation, we educate them on the subject. Just as clothing creates or ruins an image, your speech can do the same. It can prevent upward mobility in the working world."

Because of television's powerful influence, the typical Brooklyn accent is gradually fading away. Some day it may be as fond a memory as Ebbets Field.

Stained Glass

STAIRWAYS TO HEAVEN

Brooklyn's history of liberalism and intellectual free-dom, dating back to its tolerant Dutch settlers, con-tinues to make the borough a welcoming place to religious groups of every persuasion, from the main-stream to the idiosyncratic, from those who follow the Bible—or simply concoct their own.

When it comes to a house of worship Brooklyn is unique among American cities: there are about 1,300 churches, temples, mosques, and centers for acknowledging the god of one's choice. The diverse religions and sects steadfastly try to preserve a live-and-let-live, or pray-and-let-pray, philosophy among their congre-gations, regardless of diet, garb, or hairstyles within their communities. Some of the religious enclaves, however, are known for their insularity, which can result in neighborhood tensions and conflicts. And there are indeed some spiritual leaders or their flocks who practice bigotry and superstition when they preach their dog-mas. The "melting pot" of America that Brooklyn symbolizes, a blur of class and color, has made a sometimes benign and some-times tense mix of rosaries and yarmulkes.

Catholics may attend mass in 17 languages at 124 churches scat-tered throughout Brooklyn, including Ukrainian and Greek Ortho-dox. Approximately 640,500 Brooklynites identify themselves as Catholic and 400,000 observe the rituals of Judaism, the most visi-ble being the Satmar Hasidim in Williamsburg and the Lubavitch Hasidim in Crown Heights. There are 100,000 Muslims following the teachings of Mohammed and 12,000 Jehovah's Witnesses be-lieving that an Apocalypse will transform the earth into paradise for those who deflect the devil.

Nearly 100,000 Quakers, Unitarians, Pentecostals, Seventh-Day Adventists, Methodists, Lutherans, and any other Protestant de-nomination that you can name also gather in their own 288 churches. (Brooklyn old-timers remember Anniversary Day when all the Protestant Sunday schools of the city paraded up and down Clinton Street to the music of bands.) The Concord Baptist Church at 833 Marcy Avenue in Bedford–Stuyvesant is celebrated as the

Flatbush Reformed Dutch Church, built in 1793–98, the oldest of three churches built according to the mandate of Governor Peter Stuyvesant.
Photograph © Tony Velez

Who'll Buy?

On a bright sunny Sunday in June 1861, there wasn't even standing room at the Plymouth Church. Word had leaked out that the Reverend had something up his clerical sleeve. To dramatize the humiliation of a slave auction, he ordered a mulatto slave girl named Sarah to the pulpit. "She has been sold by her own father to be sent south. She was bought by a Federal slave-dealer for $1,200, and he has offered to give you the opportunity of purchasing her freedom."

In the spellbinding voice of an auctioneer, he went on, "Look at this remarkable commodity—who bids? Now look at her trim figure and wavy hair! How much do you bid for them? She is sound in mind and limb, I'll warrant her! Who bids? Her feet and hands—hold them out, Sarah—are small and finely formed. What do you bid for her?" The sanctuary was filled with gasps and sobs. "Come, now," Beecher rumbled, "we are selling this woman, don't you want her? Pass the baskets and let us see!"

Women tossed rings and necklaces and bracelets into the baskets. Men reached into pockets and wallets, stuffing the baskets with paper bills. When the collection was over and the baskets were placed before Beecher and the slave girl, he announced in a hushed tone, "There, Sarah, you are free."

As the Civil War approached, the admission of Kansas to the Union as a free or slave state was vehemently debated. Beecher thundered from his pulpit that a rifle was as good "to send as a Bible." His parishioners brought rifles, which were known as "Beecher Bibles," to the church and they were dispatched to Kansas. "Slavery is wrong," insisted Beecher. "Slavery shall not extend. Slavery shall die."

Henry Ward Beecher selling a black woman from his pulpit as an Abolitionist demonstration of the cruelty of slavery. *Lithograph. Brooklyn College Library, Special Collections*

Plymouth Church of the Pilgrims, originally Plymouth Church, built in 1849. Henry Ward Beecher preached here from 1847 to 1887. *UPI/Bettmann*

largest black congregation in the country, with over 12,000 members. Wherever and however you choose to worship—with rousing gospel songs or a solemn requiem—you can probably find it no more than a ten-minute ride from your house.

Brooklyn's oldest church was the Flatbush Reformed Dutch, where hymns were first heard in 1654. The Episcopalians started reciting the Apostle's Creed at St. Ann's in Brooklyn Heights, where many emigrés from England were building houses shortly after the Revolutionary War; they remain influential, with over thirty-five churches. The Presbyterians, so active in the Revolutionary War that in England it was called a "Presbyterian Rebellion," established the first of twenty-five parishes in 1822.

PREACHER BEECHER

For forty years Henry Ward Beecher, the brother of Harriet Beecher Stowe, author of *Uncle Tom's Cabin*, was Brooklyn's most famous preacher. "Just follow the crowd," strangers eager to hear the charismatic Beecher were told on a Sunday morning. From 1847 to 1887, he drew packed houses to the Plymouth Church in Brooklyn Heights. Ferries called "Beecher boats" even brought the dedicated through rain and wind from Manhattan. Beecher, a Congregationalist minister, spoke out passionately against slavery and immorality, though later in his career a scandal arose when he was accused of seducing a friend's wife. Combining the qualities of an actor and an impresario, Beecher, with his shoulder-length gray locks, sparkling eyes, and proud head always knew how to put on a good show, whether defending himself in court or pounding the pulpit as an Abolitionist. Like some who suffer from too much religiosity, his questionable morality cast doubt on his sanctity, but his stand against slavery was sincere—and spectacular.

A REFUGE AND STRENGTH

Other Brooklyn churches also fought the slave traffic and became "terminals" in the famous Underground Railroad. The Protestant churches of Brooklyn became, in fact, a refuge, comfort, and strength to many blacks. Methodists were so hospitable that, initially, blacks adopted their faith. Older blacks still gather in Methodist, Baptist, Presbyterian, and Catholic churches, where the membership is either integrated or all black. And from these churches have come celebrated black ministers, such as Thomas S. Harten who presided at the Holy Trinity Baptist Church at 10 Ralph Avenue in Bed–Stuy. During the 1920s and 30s, he led protest marches, organized an F.D.R. for President Party, and was nominated for Congress. And these ministers often espoused provocative messages. Advocating birth control in the 1920s, the Reverend Henry Hugh Proctor of Nazarene Congregation Unified Church of Christ advised, "It is not the divine objective to increase the population of heaven, but to improve the breed on earth."

This page, opposite, and overleaf
Easter Sunday in Bedford–Stuyvesant.
Photograph © David Lee

148

150

151

ALLAH BE PRAISED

Today there is a decline in church membership among blacks, particularly among the young. In the throes of identity crises, the young reject traditional dogma and, in looking for an experience that relates to the roots of their African ancestors, are turning to the Islamic, or Moslem, faith. Various Moslem groups populate Brooklyn, from cozy middle-class suburban areas that resemble a TV scene on the *Bill Cosby Show* to the bleak housing projects and crumbling tenements that evoke the devastation of a Third World country.

The most visible Moslem sects are the orthodox Sunni and the moderate or reformed Moorish. They both proclaim Allah as God, believe Mohammed was his messenger, and accept the Koran as sacred scripture. There have been militant, nationalistic anti-white groups that bear the Islamic banner, though the ancient belief of Islam is one of peace and racial equality.

The Reverend Proctor had a dream that never came to pass in his lifetime: he wanted to build a vast Nazarene Temple—the center for the life of his people—where they could find a bank, pharmacy, restaurant, grocery store, laundry, and so on. But today the Moslems own their own businesses, bake their bread, sew their clothing, may live together in one housing development or own blocks of row houses. So Proctor's dream *is* a reality, though slightly revised and under another religion.

Since "crack," the powerful cocaine derivative, was being sold in abandoned buildings of Bed–Stuy, a mosque on Fulton Street organized a round-the-clock street patrol to protect merchants and residents. Even the Concord Baptist Church in Bed–Stuy hired a Moslem-owned security company to protect parishioners. Drive through Bushwick on a moonless night and you'll see spectral figures—men in white robes—serenely standing on street corners, where German immigrants, Lutherans and Catholics who worked in the Brooklyn breweries, lived a hundred years ago. The robed guardians of Bushwick, who give the streets a surreal other-world atmosphere by night, are Moslems who belong to the Ansara group.

Radical elements first gave the Moslems visibility, but in Brooklyn, many have quietly been praying to Allah for years. The grandfather of Joseph Jeffries-El founded a Moorish congregation in Brownsville back in 1932, and today a small group of young people, between the ages of twenty and thirty, worship in a Brownsville mosque on New Lots Avenue where Joseph Jeffries-El is the grand sheikh—the equivalent, he says, to a minister or rabbi. The "El" appendage to the name of this third-generation Moorish-American is the Islamic word for God. Moslem men customarily choose an

Muslims in Brooklyn. *Photograph ©
David Lee*

attribute of God and add it to their surnames such as Al-Rahman
(the beneficent) or Al-Raheem (the merciful). Women find a word
suggesting the beauty of nature or, perhaps, hyphenate the name of
a prophet's wife.

"It has not been easy to be black and live in America," says Joseph Jeffries-El. "We are all searching for our identity, and a Moslem name often helps us view ourselves in a larger world." At his
services the men don red fezzes and the women wear turbans of
white or red (the Moorish flag is red and green). At a Sunni mosque
the men wear turbans and the women are often veiled. Kneeling on
prayer rugs at Friday noon worship, the Moslem men and women
pray in Arabic in separate rooms. Though they join each other in
one room for the sermon, they sit on separate sides of the aisle.
Mixing of the sexes is considered a distraction from being "at one
with God and nature." There's chanting instead of singing, and the
faithful in Bed–Stuy, Brownsville, Bushwick, and Crown Heights
may stay at home to pray. In their religious world there's no monthly meatloaf supper—or Bingo game. The various sects have formed
their own tightly knit communities, which also help with jobs and
education, so the mosque does not function as a fellowship hall.

The worshipers have dreams of visiting Mecca in Saudi Arabia. Kaa-bah, they explain, the holy shrine of Islam, is in Mecca, and Moslems are required to go there at least once. To some, Islam is too restrictive and ascetic a faith—if it is seen only as a vehicle for spirituality and not militant nationalism. Drugs and drink are not acceptable, and some young blacks find that praying five times a day—at dawn, noon, in the afternoon and evening, and before bed—demands a fervent discipline that isn't always easy to practice.

BY CANDLELIGHT

Historically, Jews were often forbidden to worship publicly. The oldest orthodox congregation in Brooklyn first met in private homes in 1848. The first synagogue opened its doors twelve years later. But today, the Jews in the news in Brooklyn are the Lubavitcher Hasidim who cluster in Crown Heights. Ultra-orthodox, they do not send their children to public schools and seldom watch commercial television. But the Hasidim do not consider themselves insular. "We find in the Talmud," says one rabbi, "that the purpose of the Jew is to take the secular and make it holy." A few miles away, the community of Williamsburg, with a population of 64,000, is divided between Hispanics and Hasidim. There have been repeated skirmishes between the two. The Satmar Hasidim in Williamsburg have their own bus system (the men and women ride separately), their own crime patrols, ambulances, shops, and stores. The Hasidim are warned on billboards, in Yiddish, about "the evils of television," which they view as a destructive influence, a notion with which sociologists are coming to agree.

The Hasidim, who revere the Bible as the Will of God, strictly observe their Saturday Sabbath: they will not travel or conduct business and always they "keep kosher," which, among other restrictions, prohibits the eating of meat and dairy products together. There are, of course, many less orthodox Jews who follow the teachings of the Conservative and Reform synagogues. It's even possible to find a handful of black Jews who trace their ancestry back to King Solomon.

A PEACEABLE KINGDOM

Door-to-door, house-to-house advisories on Heaven and Hell are the work of the Jehovah's Witnesses, a multiracial evangelistic sect with three million members that has its world headquarters in Brooklyn Heights. The old Squibb Building, once a pharmaceutical plant, now has huge black lettering stating The Watchtower on its façade fronting Manhattan, so it's impossible to miss when you're crossing the Bridge into Brooklyn.

Hasidic Jews in Williamsburg.
Photograph © David Lee

The Watchtower and Bible Society, the name of the sect's corporation, was established in Brooklyn Heights in 1909. Brooklyn offered then, and for many years thereafter, an international port. The Watchtower Society, which prints its literature for worldwide circulation, wanted access to shipping lines. For the Jehovah's Witnesses—in Brooklyn—are not just a religion; they're an industry. Today there are over three million Witnesses, of all colors, in the world, and their two publications, *The Watchtower* and *Awake!*, are distributed to an estimated twenty-three million. The society began buying property in the Heights over thirty years ago when brownstones and apartment buildings were up for grabs. It now owns property last assessed at $25 million, which includes former hotels, a slew of brownstones and offices, and a factory complex that ranges over five city blocks. Ironically, one purchase was the four-story residence of Henry Ward Beecher at 124 Columbia Heights. It's now the residence of thirty Witness employees. The Witnesses want to keep expanding. They strongly believe that growth is a reflection of God's will.

Housed in hotels and brownstones are 2,500 staff members—essentially workers—who receive free room and board, plus a $35 a month allowance, $45 a month for transportation costs, and $360 a year for clothing. Many are between the ages of nineteen and thirty-five, but some are well into their sixties, secure in the knowledge that the society will always care for them. The young volunteers learn about graphics, book-binding, and printing. The society produces over two million Bibles a year and countless illustrated tracts. The volunteers study doctrine, public speaking, and Bible lessons. Communal dining rooms prepare food grown on upstate farms. At World Headquarters, a family spirit pervades: the Witnesses, who descend on the Heights from across the country, but mostly from the Midwest, pray together, eat together, and team up to ring doorbells, eager to tell others about their heavenly Father.

Their movement, which has predicted the end of the world more than a half-dozen times, stresses that 144,000 will go to heaven. (This number from the Book of Revelation, 7:4.) Ultimately an Apocalypse will transform the rubble left on earth into paradise for those who've kept the devil at bay. Rather than risk God's disapproval, the Witnesses do not accept blood transfusions. They will not salute the flag of any nation (an un-Christian image), and many died during World War II in concentration camps for refusal to acknowledge the Nazi banner. In Brooklyn a family spirit pervades their peaceable kingdom as the Witnesses try to remove themselves from the degrading qualities of life—most particularly violence and vulgarity.

World Headquarters of Jehovah's Witnesses in Brooklyn Heights.
Jehovah's Witnesses

Mexican Festival of Guadalupe in
Williamsburg. *Photograph © Tony Velez*

Christmas service in All Saints Roman
Catholic Church in Williamsburg.
Photograph © David Lee

THREE WISE WOMEN

The Roman Catholic Church does not ordain women as priests, and
the Vatican isn't likely to change its doctrine, but in Brooklyn for
five years there were three nuns who not only organized the Sunday
masses, but also preached—maybe twice a month. Sisters Peggy
Lynch, Mary Lou Lyons, and Sheila Buhse—who all speak Spanish—were pioneers in a parish with many Hispanics who felt their
presence was the best thing that's happened in a long time. And,
although the three energetic nuns may sound like characters from
an updated version of the movie *The Bells of St. Mary's*, they were
not conceived by any script writer. All Saints Roman Catholic
Church at 115 Throop Avenue in the Williamsburg section was
without a full-time priest. Others didn't speak Spanish. The neighborhood was considered "troubled." The cavernous church, built
almost one hundred years ago with green marble columns and
stained-glass windows, seemed on the verge of closing. Then, the
three nuns, members of the Dominican Sisters on Long Island,
were given a chance to see what they could do, and it turned out to
be a lot.

To the Spanish-speaking congregation, the nuns brought a positive, humanizing dignity. They also found that many women in the

church preferred to take their problems to another woman rather than a church father. The nuns felt they were sharing their gifts with people hungry for a grain of truth and love in a neighborhood of sterile housing projects and abandoned lots filled with trash where drugs are secretly sold. Before departing for another parish, Sister Sheila said, "Our aim is to get our members into responsible roles here. We are their servants, and may come and go. But *they* are the church."

THE AMEN CORNER

Dig around a bit in Brooklyn's religious past, and you never know what might turn up, or who. Pat Robertson, the preacher who would be president, formally declared his 1988 candidacy in Brooklyn, in front of a Bedford–Stuyvesant brownstone. In the early 60s, the dimple-cheeked evangelist had spent two months there because, he said, the Lord had called him to minister to the poor. And in that same brownstone, he learned that a rundown television station in Portsmouth, Virginia, was for sale, and he decided to "claim it for the Lord." The residents reacted with bemusement to the founder of a Fundamentalist broadcasting empire returning to the neighborhood. The band played "Glory, Hallelujah," and cries of "Amen!" were mixed with "Go home, Pat."

Hands held high, his message to Brooklyn was, "God bless you."

Sing Out, Sweet Land

The Chapin brothers—Harry, Tom, and Steve—first performed as a group, singing "This Land Is Your Land" at Grace Church at 254 Hicks Street in Brooklyn Heights. This was in the late 50s; and Tom—singer, songwriter, guitarist, and actor—was then only twelve. "I was dragged, kicking and screaming, by my mother to my first choir rehearsal when I was a child," he recalls fondly, "and I stayed in the choir until I went to college. Without Grace Episcopal Church, and the music opportunities there, it's hard to know what would have happened to us."

The church, so close to the Chapin home on Hicks Street, was founded by old Brooklyn society. At its Young People's Fellowship proper girls met proper boys. "There were tea dances," Tom Chapin remembers, "and we had to get dressed up in suits that never quite fit, with white collars and white gloves." The church had some very wealthy members. The Chapins, Tom says, "were poor but presentable."

The Chapin brothers (Harry, the oldest and creator of story-songs, was struck and killed by an unlicensed driver in the early 80s) credit the church, rather than a cabaret or vaudeville show, for catapulting them to the stage of Carnegie Hall. It was the beginning of the folk era. And they were three clean-cut fellas, in button-down shirts, who projected a sunny image straight from the heartland of America. "I do think of Brooklyn as a heartland," Tom Chapin says, "and its tolerance *is* reflected in the openness of its churches and welcoming religions. Grace Church was a memorable part of my life."

The "musical" Chapin Brothers. From the top, Tom, Steve, and Harry. Summer 1962. *Courtesy Elspeth Hart*

161

Pleasures and Pastimes

CONEY ISLAND!

Magical words for millions around the world! A romantic paradise of cheap thrills n' chills, Coney Island was made legendary through music, the movies, Broadway shows, novels, photographs, and word-of-mouth from those who went there and returned home *alive* with stories to tell of airplane swings, giant roller coasters, fun houses, shoot-the-chutes, sky-high Ferris wheels, bearded gentlewomen and the Illustrated (tattooed) Man. America's most famed amusement park has gone through many changes, from a corrupt and lawless turf at the end of the last century to a daredevil playground by the sea that reached its peak of popularity during World War II. Today, despite crime, decay, and gaudy honky-tonk, Coney Island attracts hordes of people of all social strata, who want to imagine the past delights of Coney or seek out new sensations on the six-mile-long sandbar facing the Atlantic Ocean.

During the winter months, Coney has the atmosphere of a ghost town that could be blown away. The shops and stands along the boardwalk are shuttered. The silent roller coaster tracks look twisted, as if by a tornado. The unmoving Ferris wheel is a circular skeleton in space. The horses on the merry-go-round are frozen. A few stragglers meander along the beach: they could be homeless, lovers, or undercover cops. On side streets littered with broken glass anonymous cars stop momentarily, then speed away, a drug deal completed. Coney seems to die in winter, when there are no pleasure-seekers or lordly carnival barkers crowding a landscape of hideous housing projects surreal in their sterility, where dreams do not survive. But, come summer, with the smell of cotton candy, hot dogs, candied apples, and buttered popcorn, along with the sweat from tanned and oiled bodies, and tangled limbs that expose all, on the beach and the boardwalk, the faded resort lights up like a firecracker, bathing itself in brilliant colors and bringing alive the past. Coney Island still has a powerful hold on the imagination.

The Dutch farmers who first settled the seaside land found themselves squeezed in the mid-1800s by cottages, then mansions, bath-

Parachute Jump, Steeplechase Park, Coney Island. *Brooklyn Public Library, Brooklyn Collection*

Bathers at Coney Island. *Photograph © David Lee*

The immense spiderweb of the
Wonderwheel in Coney Island.

Photograph © Tony Velez

houses, and hotels that lured affluent merrymakers in boats from Manhattan. Soon trains and boulevards reached Coney Island, bringing the "sporting set," keen on prizefighting, horse racing, then speed-car racing in Sheepshead and Gravesend Bay. Dance halls, saloons, and gambling dens brought out "ladies of the evening" and bigshots who knew about the rackets. Coney's most preposterous place to spend a night or amorous afternoon hours in the 1890s was the Elephant Hotel, which was made of wood and tin and looked like an elephant, tusks and all. Rooms could be booked in the head, stomach, or parts elsewhere. It was not a hostel for families. In 1896, "The Colossus of Architecture" was destroyed by fire.

Fleeing jail, the political thug "Boss" Tweed ran to a Coney Island fancy house. The militant Carrie Nation, who extolled temperance, campaigned at Coney to save souls from Sodom-by-the-Sea. Revelers in the beachfront bars were having, always, too good a time. Over the years everybody from the nineteenth-century statesman Daniel Webster to the musician Woody Guthrie were amused by Coney Island. In the late 1890s "Diamond Jim" Brady, who made a fortune in the railroad business, sauntered on the

Brighton Beach and Boardwalk, Coney Island, c. 1905. *Photograph George P. Hall & Son. New-York Historical Society*

boardwalk wearing diamond-studded sandals. Celebrated for his gems as well as his girth, "Diamond Jim" once went for a swim and began floating on his back. Friends on the beach gleefully shouted that Fire Island had become unmoored and was drifting out to sea. His favorite arm-piece was the musical comedy star and glamorous sex symbol of the period Lillian Russell. Their affair was strictly platonic as diamonds were *his* best friend, but he nonetheless installed her in a Mediterranean villa in Bay Ridge (now a Catholic girls' school at 9901 Shore Road). When not dining at home, they'd catch all eyes in the posh hotels, such as the Victoria Chateau in Gravesend Bay—she for her beauty and hourglass figure, he for his diamonds and fat. Brady liked his oysters with clams and his steaks smothered with veal cutlets.

After World War I, Coney's music halls were packed for such vaudevillians as Eddie Cantor, who rhythmically rolled his banjo eyes, and Jimmy Durante, who wriggled his endearing "schnozzola" while exclaiming, *"Everybody wants ta get into de act!"* Broadway producers of the 20s and early 30s liked to use Coney's theaters for tryouts. Moss Hart's *Once in a Lifetime,* his first play and collaboration with George S. Kaufman, was booked at Coney before con-

"Lagoon and Shoot the Chutes."
Postcard from Souvenir of Coney Island, *published by the American Art Publishing Co., N.Y. New-York Historical Society*

Lagoon and Chute the Chutes.

Diamond Jim Brady proudly flashed his jewels while consuming oysters, lobster, and steak at the seaside resort. *The Bettmann Archive*

Lillian Russell, who immortalized the hourglass figure, reveled in a frolic at Coney Island. *The Bettmann Archive*

fronting critics across the river. Theaters and dance halls echoed to the sounds of ragtime, Viennese waltzes, hot-cha jazz, and John Philip Sousa's band. A young actor-acrobat from London named Archie Leach earned his bread and butter by walking on stilts on the Boardwalk. He rose even higher as a Hollywood actor with the name of Cary Grant.

The novelist and cultural gadfly Carl Van Vechten writes of a trip to Coney during the 20s with some society swells: "At last the towers and minarets and scenic railways of Coney Island came into view in the sonorous light; then, the wide strip of ocean, the beach strewn with refuse and bathers. A mechanical piano wailed out 'Say It with Music' a quarter tone off key. Barkers everywhere: 'Now, ladies and gentlemen, I have the honor to present this afternoon this little lady here on my right, the Princess Sesame, considered by many to be the GREATEST LIVING EXPONENT of oriental harem dancing. INSIDE THIS TENT... the Sicilian shimmy dagger dance!'" And amid the shooting galleries, Venetian canals, and pig slides, the society swells agreed that Coney was all of life and most of death, the pagan idea of heaven and the Christian conception of hell. Balloons and kewpie dolls, Eskimo pies and pretzels, and the sideshows—ah yes! Where else could you see sword swallowers, the Wild Man of Borneo, the Rrrrrrrrrussian Cossack with a hook passed through his tongue, or a nymphet who wrapped a forty-pound boa constrictor around her waist and defied it to crush her! Today, decades later, a Snake Woman and Sword Swallower are still part of Coney's hurdy-gurdy freak shows, but Dreamland, with its village of three hundred midgets, is gone, and so is Luna Park, with its "hhurrrrry, hurrrrrry" Trip to the Moon and North Pole rides. Only an amusement park called Astroland preserves Coney Island's thrill-a-minute reputation.

Carl Van Vechten sped to Coney Island in a Rolls-Royce. The great American writer Willa Cather went by boat that left from Desbrosses Street in lower Manhattan. After a shore dinner with tall steins of beer, she recalled watching a beautiful young woman risk her life for those willing to pay for viewing perilous entertainment. While a six-piece band played furiously, a balloon rose from a tent with the girl standing in the basket, "holding carelessly to one of the ropes with one hand and with the other waving to the spectators. A long rope trailed behind to keep the balloon from blowing out to sea." When the balloon began to descend the girl moved from the basket to a trapeze, "holding to the rod with both hands, keeping her body taut and her feet close together." And when the balloon touched ground, the devil-may-care balloonist was given a bouquet of artificial flowers.

The revue artist Beatrice Lillie, who convulsed audiences with her tongue twister about two dozen double damask dinner napkins, often went to Coney Island when appearing on Broadway in the 1950s. Her favorite date was the child actor Brandon de Wilde. She ventured into the Tunnel of Love with him but put her foot down when it came to climbing aboard the heart-pounding, body-shattering Cyclone, Coney's celebrated roller coaster. Opening nights provided Bea Lillie with enough terror.

Young, curvaceous hellers in tights no longer descend in balloons for cheering crowds, and the Parachute Jump, which took the adventurous 260 feet high in ski-lift chairs and then floated them in midair—a big hit after the 1939 World's Fair—is a memory, too, but still visible at Coney Island as a rusted relic. But the stupendous

Former Coney Island entertainers Eddie Cantor and Jimmy Durante at the reopening of the Loew's Ziegfeld Theatre in New York, April 1933. *UPI/Bettmann*

"The Most Delightful Route to the Sea Shore." *Lithographic poster. New-York Historical Society, The Bella C. Landauer Collection*

Overleaf
Luna Park, Coney Island, 1911. *Photograph George P. Hall & Son. New-York Historical Society*

old Cyclone still exists. It takes riders on a harrowing 85-foot plunge and hits 60 miles an hour.

Up, up, up slowly climbs the Cyclone, giving riders in the three-car train at Astroland a breathtaking view of the Atlantic Ocean and more than two miles of boardwalk, a ribbon running down to Brighton Beach. The Cyclone, awarded official status by the Landmarks Preservation Commission, seems to putter along the wooden tracks as it climbs the first alpine hill. Reaching the top, it heaves a choked-up sigh, then hurtles down the first drop, a gasping heart-in-yer-mouth drop. The next minute-and-a-half is nonstop terror as the Cyclone careens up, down, and around six turns at breakneck speed.

For those who prefer milder titillations, there's always the Wonder Wheel. The dangling "cabins" swing nervously back and forth on this Ferris wheel that reaches an altitude of 135 feet.

It's always best to eat *after* sampling Coney's dipsy-doodle "rides."

Over the years the number of sensualists converging on Surf Avenue, the main strip, and the sand itself have varied from around a hundred thousand to nearly two million on a steamy Fourth of July in the late 1980s when crowds gathered for the annual hot dog eating contest sponsored by Coney's famous eatery, Nathan's. A two-time winner was a young man named Jay Green who gulped down (three bites a frank) almost sixteen hot dogs in twelve minutes. "there's no preparing for this contest," he said modestly, "you just got to eat like a pig."

Humans and sideshow freaks aside, Coney Island is also famous for other kinds of animals—those who make a splash at the New York Aquarium. The compound, spread over fourteen acres, harbors beluga whales, sharks, penguins, sea bass, sea turtles, eels, seals, piranhas, anemones, sea lions, and dolphins. Some disport in the 1,000-seat Marine Stadium. It was rumored that a 40-foot humpback whale, cruising recently in New York Harbor, was in search of work at the stadium. He got lost around Red Hook and was last sighted near the Verrazano Bridge, heading out to sea.

PARKWAY TO THE PARK

From Coney Island to more bucolic pleasures, take Eastern Parkway, which suggests the Champs Elysées in Paris or Unter den Linden in Berlin before World War II. This wide, two-mile stretch was designed in 1870 by Frederick Law Olmsted and Calvert Vaux, the two distinguished landscape architects who designed Central Park in New York. Eastern Parkway has been landmarked as the first parkway in the nation. Its designers left an even larger legacy in

Bathers build their own shelter on the beach at Coney Island. *Photograph © David Lee*

The Cyclone, Coney Island. *Photograph © David Lee*

Equestrian group at the Ocean Park entrance to Prospect Park. *New-York Historical Society*

Overleaf
Nathan's Famous, Coney Island.
Nathan's Famous

Brooklyn. Besides Eastern Parkway, they created Grand Army Plaza, Ocean Parkway, and their chef d'oeuvre—Prospect Park, a stirring sweep of greenery that refreshed the cityscape with natural beauty.

Eastern Parkway, completed a few years after the park's opening, is a boulevard bounded by grassy malls and carriage ways, where families, children, and couples once meandered past mansions, town houses, and the Brooklyn Museum. On balmy afternoons, they'd repose on parkway benches and watch the passing parade of people on foot or in horse-and-buggies and, later, Model T's. At dusk the lamps along Eastern Parkway cast a golden glow along the inviting boulevard lined with Dutch elm trees. After some years of neglect, Eastern Parkway is being restored to its original brightness, but progress is caught up in contractual snarls. The roadway, sidewalks, and grassy areas are gradually looking greener and smoother because of new plantings and resurfacing. Electric lanterns, evoking the turn-of-the-century lamps, are planned to light up the sky. The parkway is moving into the present.

The arch that begins the Parkway in Grand Army Plaza stands as the imposing gateway to Prospect Park, with its 526 acres of slopes and hills and ridges and meadows—the leavings of glaciers from the Ice Age. It remains an idyllic spot to picnic, jog, horseback ride, gaze into a pond or lake, ice skate, listen to an outdoor concert,

The Boathouse in Prospect Park, built in 1905. *Photograph George P. Hall. New-York Historical Society*

inspect a zoo, play baseball, or quote poetry if it's a romantic occasion. Walkways and bridle paths and tunnels curl around a forest of whispering elms and oaks—some three hundred years old. Though Coney Island became world famous for its razzmatazz pleasures, Prospect Park is cherished for pastoral pastimes.

The woods and glades reek of history. A crucial struggle in the Revolutionary War was fought at a site marked Battle Pass. And the Lefferts Homestead, built in 1783 and now standing in the park, was given to Brooklyn by the descendants of Lieutenant Peter Lefferts, whose first house was razed by the British. The Dutch Colonial farmhouse—a museum of period furniture and design—recalls to life the early eighteenth century with such authenticity that you would not be surprised to find a dimpled Dutch Colonist preparing pumpkin soup in the kitchen. The house isn't an amusement park replica: it's the real thing. Park architects Olmsted and Vaux would appreciate the humanizing presence of the historic house within their sylvan glades.

Olmstead, who grew up during the Industrial Revolution, perceived that the clock could never be turned back to the simplicity of a quiet, friendly rural time. Both he and his partner saw Prospect Park as a kind of preservation society. It wasn't just to provide "an opportunity for getting fresh air and exercise," explained Olmsted. "The main object is to produce a certain influence in the minds of people and through this to make life in the city healthier and happier." The two visionaries foresaw the arrival of the urban asphalt jungle. Olmsted, who had seen the gardens and parks of Europe, was particularly keen on capturing memories of parks seen in England, such as Victoria Park in London and Birkenhead near Liverpool. But the park must not only preserve; it must also be, he felt, a civilized refuge that blended into the city.

The highest point in the park, where Sunday carriage drives were a desirable outing for ladies holding parasols and gentlemen in top hats, is Lookout Hill (north of the boathouse), another reminder of Early Americana. On the hill is the Maryland Monument, designed by Stanford White in 1895, a tribute to a Maryland regiment whose courageous tactics during the Revolutionary War allowed Washington's troops to retreat safely from the befuddled British. Atop Lookout Hill, you can look over the panorama of Brooklyn to the harbor and ocean—a setting that, even today, seems created for a children's pop-up book, unreal but ever so vivid.

SANCTUARY OF SPIRITs

"Only the Dead Know Brooklyn," claimed the novelist Thomas Wolfe, whose short story of that title was written when he lived in Brooklyn Heights during the 1930s. There was just too much to the sprawling, raucous borough, he suggested, so until you were immersed in its earth, with the soil of the borough seeping into your body and brain, you'd never really understand its passionate personality. Thomas Wolfe may have had in mind the inhabitants of

Entrance to Green-Wood Cemetery, the Fort Hamilton Parkway Gate and Gatehouse, built in 1875, designed by Richard M. Upjohn. Photograph Byron. Museum of the City of New York, The Byron Collection

Lola Montez, from an early daguerreotype, taken during her stay in America, early 1850s. The Bettmann Archive

Lola's Last Dance

Maria Dolores Eliza Rosanna Gilbert is the name on the small stone. But the *jolie femme*, whose liaisons with King Ludwig of Bavaria, Franz Liszt, Prince Henry of Reuss, and Alexander Dumas were notorious, called herself Lola Montez. Her father was the great Spanish toreador Montez, said Lola, and her mother was Queen Maria Christina. Pure poppycock! She was just a poor and pretty girl from Ireland who ran away from home with her mother's lover. By the mid-nineteenth century she was dancing on the stages of Europe—Warsaw, Dresden, Bonn, Paris. When gold was discovered in California, Lola was in San Francisco doing her Spider Dance. Attired in tights and a tutu of a skirt, she'd twist and turn, shaking out rubber spiders from the folds of her flouncy garment, which she'd then stab with her stiletto-heeled slippers. It is not known whether Lola Montez visited Brooklyn before her trip to Green-Wood. But when she died in 1861 in poverty at the age of 41 in Manhattan, a woman who remembered the vivacious Lola Montez from Europe found space for her in the family plot in Green-Wood, according to Marge Ward of Brooklyn, who for many years conducted tours of the cemetery with her late husband, editor-teacher Bill Ward. Without Marge Ward as guide, you'd never notice the Gilbert grave.

Green-Wood Cemetery. Though the unknown and the forgotten are among the 530,000 buried in Green-Wood, the Egyptian-styled mausoleums and Gothic tombs also commemorate a Who's Who of names linked not only to Brooklyn but also to the emergence of America. Imagine tales told on a silvery night if, up from the graves of Green-Wood arose Horace Greeley, Alice Lee Roosevelt, Samuel Morse, Louis Comfort Tiffany, Lola Montez, Henry Ward Beecher, "Boss" (William Marcy) Tweed, and Leonard Jerome, the financier who was Winston Churchill's grandfather.

Located in the Sunset Park area, between Park Slope and Bay Ridge, the cemetery is a gracious spread of hillocks and knolls where notable Brooklyn families—among them Livingston, Bergen, Cortelyou, Pierrepont—repose under obelisks, temples, and statues of the muses and divinities. The cemetery was the inspiration of Henry Pierrepont, whose father made a fortune in the borough with his gin distillery. Young Henry decided that Brooklyn should have a classical cemetery like Mount Auburn in Cambridge, Massachusetts, that would offer beauty for the bereaved as well as something special: a mixture of art and architecture within a primeval forest. Green-Wood, which opened in 1840, would be more than a cemetery—it would be a sanctuary to ennoble the spirits of the living, an idea that reached baroque extremes a century later at Forest Lawn Memorial Park in Glendale, California.

And so, Green-Wood, with its archangels and cherubs, made of marble, plaster, and cement, became a "sight to see." In the nineteenth century, the sensibilities of Sunday strollers were presumably enhanced by leisurely walks over the 20 miles of winding path; families had sedate picnics on the grass, and lovers went boating on the lake. To preserve an atmosphere of dignity, you could not shoot fowl or race horses. Today the philosophy of mourning and aesthetics have dramatically changed since the Victorian era. And there are no people lolling on the grass or idling in boats. Green-Wood is an environment of sculptural treasures and melancholy hosts. It remains, as *The New York Times* reflected long ago, "one of the institutions to be served up to all strangers, and no guest has been courteously entertained until he has been driven through its winding avenues and looked down upon the bay and the city from its commanding heights."

BOOKWORMS

Whispered voices, hushed rooms.

The sixty public libraries in Brooklyn have been a retreat and resource for thousands of immigrants learning a new language in a new world, and their children, since the first library opened in the

Gilded reliefs by C. Paul Jennewein and screen by Thomas H. Jones at the entrance of the Main Library of the Brooklyn Public Library, built in 1941. *Library of Congress, Washington, D.C.*

early nineteenth century. Henry Miller, one of America's most significant writers, recalled that a branch in Brooklyn Heights was "a morgue of a place, but filled with treasures . . . often it was impossible to read, the place *was just too wonderful.*" The novelist Betty Smith remembered her branch as a shabby place, but to her it was beautiful. It reminded her of being in a church. She liked the smell of the books and inked stamping pads better than she liked "the smell of burning incense at high mass." She thought all the books in the world were there, and she planned, as a child, to read all the books in the world. The distinctive journalist Pete Hamill wrote that for a long time his library was "the true center of the world."

The libraries, an escape from tenements and cramped apartments, a "second home" for so many, particularly before the arrival of television, still have a life of their own, with about nine million "check-outs" registered each year, though today video cassettes of film classics and documentaries are also on the shelves. "A child in the library—any child—presents us with a challenge," says Larry Brandwein, director of the Brooklyn library system. "It is up to us to show them that the library is a good place to be, a place where wonders can be unlocked and new worlds explored, a place to be revisited for the rest of their lives." In the 1980s, when the libraries faced crippling budget cuts proposed by the mayor of New York, 75,000 Brooklynites signed protest petitions within weeks. The budget was reduced but not devastated. "Hail the library," Brooklynites cheered.

The central library at the main entrance of Prospect Park is a building of elegant Art Deco persuasion, welcoming rather than awesome in its decorative luster. Initially planned as a Victorian structure, its construction was stopped by World War I and the De-

Isador Rabi, Nobel Prize–winning physicist. *AP/Wide World Photos*

Old World/New World

Isidor Isaac Rabi, a pioneer in exploring the atom, won the Nobel Prize in Physics in 1944. Rabi immigrated with his family to America from Austria–Hungary at the turn of the century and grew up in the Brownsville section of Brooklyn. "Had we stayed in Europe, I probably would have become a tailor like my father," he said. Rabi graduated from Manual Training High School, studied at Cornell, and received his doctorate at Columbia University where he joined the faculty. Recalling his thrilling discovery of the Brooklyn Public Library as a child, he once observed, "The librarian made me read to her from one of the books I was borrowing to prove I could read before she let me leave." An omnivorous reader, he continued, "I turned away from the Old World. I realized I had to be an American, not a Jewish–American. In all my reading, I tried to become an American. I read a tremendous amount of colonial history. It takes a person like me to really understand what a wonderful country America is."

Fiddlers and Flutists Afloat

Under the Brooklyn Bridge at the old Fulton Landing, on Thursday evenings and Sunday afternoons, young and old, attired in whatever feels comfortable, converge on a former coffee barge anchored in the East River. For music lovers who crave intimacy and warmth the floating concert hall known as Bargemusic easily rivals the recital rooms at Carnegie Hall and Lincoln Center. Attending a concert is like stepping into a storybook. The little "houseboat," paneled in cherrywood with a fireplace and bay windows, faces the Manhattan skyline. Cheese and crackers, cookies, and jug wine are enjoyed on deck during intermission. There's a relaxed camaraderie among the award-winning musicians and symphony soloists who revel in the opportunity to put together a program of Liszt and Beethoven.

The devoted audience of 150 sometimes sit on the very edges of their folding chairs, especially if the lulling river has a swift current. The Dutch writer-critic Felix Eijgenraam of Holland's top newspaper, *NRC Handelsblad*, explained to readers: "You have to forget about Manhattan and cross the East River... the musicians are world-class... the concert I am attending is unforgettable. Every now and then police sirens can be heard coming from the Brooklyn Bridge. Passing vessels cause a strong rocking motion of the barge, and, when a tugboat passes very close by, the sheets of the music flutter off the music stands. Between an andante and an allegro the tiny podium, creaking audibly, gets a well-aimed kick from Ik-Hwan Bae (the artistic director) to straighten it up. It's all makeshift, but nowhere can you hear music that sounds better than here."

Bargemusic, which has brought cellists and flutists to the waterfront, chasing away spooky shadows, is a dream come true for the indefatigable Olga Bloom, a superb musician herself. In the mid-70s, after the death of her husband (a violinist with Toscanini's NBC Orchestra), she mortgaged her Long Island house and bought the barge for $10,000, then had to make it shipshape for safety. "I wanted to contribute to our musical life. Chamber music should have a special environment: civilized but also cozy. There's a sameness to our schools and stores and apartment houses, and this regimentation stifles the creative spirit. But chamber music on a barge, I told my friends, could be wonderful."

Bloom, a gritty woman with luminous eyes and a hearty smile, grew up in Boston, "a child of the Depression." She received free violin lessons from a music professor at Boston University who also played with the Boston Symphony, and continued her studies—as a scholarship kid—at the New England Conservatory of Music and the Tanglewood Festival. She arrived in New York in the early 40s, "the golden years of musical comedy—shows by Cole Porter, Rodgers and Hammerstein, Irving Berlin." And she adds, "Broadway had allure then." She played in the orchestras of musicals, worked in recording studios, and did background music for movies. "The war was on, which meant that as a woman, I got opportunities that might not have been available." She later joined Stokowski's American Symphony Orchestra.

Today, Olga Bloom lives on a cobblestone street in the Red Hook section of Brooklyn, in a small house dating back to the Civil War. She was a pioneer in moving to Red Hook and in developing Bargemusic, an inspired use of the waterfront. One night, Olga and a friend remained together on the barge playing Beethoven in the late hours after a chamber concert attended by ambassadors, United Nations officials, exchange students, and her regular Brooklyn customers. Suddenly she spied—with a slight shiver—a cluster of faces pressed against the barge windows. She opened the door and beckoned a group of Hispanic youngsters inside. The music continued, from Beethoven to Stravinsky. Her visitors sat silently, transfixed.

Olga Bloom in front of Bargemusic.

Photograph © David Lee

Of Bears and Bras

The library telephone reference services answer hundreds of questions a week, from the trivial to the significant. Oddball questions, answered with aplomb, prove that even today Brooklynites are creatures of intense curiosity:

Where was the "Teddy bear" first produced and by whom?

In Brooklyn, November 18, 1902.

The creator was a man named Morris Michtom.

Who invented the brassiere?

Otto Tizling, a German-born American, made the first halter in 1910. The first elastic bra was made in 1913–1914 by the American socialite May Phelps Jacob. Under the name of Caresse Crosby, she was an impressive figure in Parisian cultural circles of the 1920s.

---

pression. Later the old designs were scrapped for the new, and the central library, designed by Alfred Morton Githing and Francis Keally, opened its bronze-and-gold doors just before World War II. Characters from American literature are celebrated in a bronze screen above the entrance by Thomas H. Jones—among them Tom Sawyer, Rip Van Winkle, Hiawatha, and Natty Bumppo. Inscribed on the façade are quotes by the world's great whose works are among the central library's 1.6 million books. A statement by the uncompromising Joseph Conrad is particularly meaningful for readers who contemplate its message today: "Of all men's creations, books are the nearest to us, for they contain our very thoughts, our ambitions, our indignations, our illusions, our fidelity to truth, and our persistent leaning toward error."

The library is not a relic or a spectacle or a site-seeing stop. It's a lively affirmation of thought and knowledge in a community, historically "bookish," that opens a vision of the universe.

DISHING IT UP

From the West Indian enclaves of Crown Heights that specialize in curries flavored with parched pepper to the Middle Eastern eateries along Atlantic Avenue that serve up Scheherazadian appetizers and the Italian bistros of Bensonhurst where the fresh pasta only needs to cook about four minutes, Brooklyn is a global banquet of feasting. The aroma of mussel soup, souvlaki, baklava, pastrami, goulash, kreplach, cuchifritos, shashlik, kjottkaker, roti—broiling, baking, or boiling—keep olfactory glands working overtime. The borough is both a haven and a kind of heaven for people who joyously forget dieting and cholesterol anxieties as they gobble up hearts of Chinese cabbage and Scandinavian sausages from among the hundreds of ethnic restaurants that give their neighborhoods essence and Brooklyn a zesty garlic-scented personality. Now vegetarian bars and others that concoct new soups and salads have also

A Middle Eastern bakery on Atlantic Avenue. *Photograph © Lisa Garcia*

opened to appease young urbanites after a jog in Prospect Park or the Saturday stroll with a perambulator.

Steeped in the nostalgia of an era when carriages and wagons jogged along the streets of downtown Brooklyn is Gage & Tollner, founded in 1879 and one of the borough's oldest restaurants. With its mahogany tables, paneled walls, and arched mirrors, it keeps the quaintness of the nineteenth century alive. Especially around eight o'clock, when the maître d' lights the thirty-six gas-fueled brass chandeliers, a ritual that interrupts the hum of conversation about the braised brisket of beef. The filmmaker Spike Lee, who provocatively satirized the Brooklyn he knows in *Do the Right Thing*, often dines by gaslight. Former mayor Ed Koch often lunched on cherrystone clams and the Charleston she-crab soup.

Bari, an Italian grocery store in Bensonhurst. *Photograph © David Lee*

Peter Luger's Steak House. *Photograph*
© *Roy Round*

Gage & Tollner's restaurant. *Photograph*
© *Tony Velez*

185

Another culinary landmark, dating back to 1887, is the Peter Luger steak house, a gemütlich bit of old Bavaria at the foot of the Williamsburg Bridge. Peter Luger fondly remembered the rowdy beer halls of his native Germany where mountainous platters were served amid warmhearted revelry and jocular waiters always knew when it was time to bring on another round of chilled beer. Though the years have rolled by, the hurly-burly elbows-on-the-table ambience remains. For those tired of mini-portions of "creative cooking" (pasta tossed with foie gras), Peter Luger's dishes up the hunkiest meal around—whopper-sized tomatoes and onions, followed by a juicy T-bone steak with French fries and creamed spinach, all washed down with imported draft beer. Only out-of-towners ask to see a menu. The Pulitzer Prize–winning poet John Ashbery often made a monthly trek from Manhattan with convivial pals just to cut into a succulent steak. And Europeans who want to sample their idea of American grub converge on the crowded dining room. The Parisian newspaper *Le Figaro* said that the most refined French palates would be happily surprised. At last count, Luger's had 47,000 charge-account customers.

Cheesecake at Junior's with sculptor Louise Bourgeois (in the cap), flanked by her assistant, Jerry Gorovoy, and collectors Ginny and Michael Williams. *Photograph © Adar Joseph*

The most popular deli in Brooklyn is Junior's, near the Brooklyn Academy of Music and the Manhattan Bridge. The 1950s Art Moderne decor provides the backdrop for a crossroads of many worlds, from locals chomping chopped liver on rye to national politicians forking the homemade cheesecake. John F. Kennedy, on the campaign trail, liked the strawberry cheesecake. During the week, seated daintily at a banquette, you are apt to see Louise Bourgeois, the grande dame of sculpture, attired in slacks, smock, and beret, quietly having a midday munch of lox and bagel. For desert she prefers the blueberry cheesecake. Like many artists who find studio space in Brooklyn more ample and more affordable than Manhattan, Bourgeois's atelier—two floors in a plant where naval uniforms were once made—is minutes away from Junior's. "The noontime activity has the drama of a theater," she says. "It takes me out of my studio, out of myself. So, I sit and watch the people."

In contrast to restaurants that celebrate Brooklyn's gilded age or the slam-bang speed of today's modernity is The River Café, which sits on a barge under the Brooklyn Bridge near Olga Bloom's Bargemusic. Serving plume de veau, sweetbreads, and salmon steak with

The River Café. *Photograph © David Lee*

187

Lundy's in Sheepshead Bay. *Photograph © Tom Madden. The New York Times*

Sundays at Lundy's

Lundy's, a sprawling stucco and red-tiled restaurant, vaguely Spanish in style, was one of Brooklyn's most famous restaurants, opening in 1934 and serving a "shore dinner" that included soup, a choice of clam, oyster, shrimp, or crabmeat cocktails, steamers, a half broiled lobster *and* a half broiled chicken, potatoes and vegetables, ice cream or pie, and coffee, tea, or milk. Until it closed in 1979, Lundy Brothers, once described as a "gastronomic Lourdes where thousands gorge in a week and miracles of gourmandise are performed," was the seafood palace of Sheepshead Bay. To it flocked generations of families who lived in Flatbush, Bensonhurst, Bay Ridge, Coney Island, and later Long Island, celebrating birthdays, anniversaries, Mother's and Father's days, or for no reason other than "eating out." Lundy's could seat 2,800 diners and easily fed about one million people a year. For some, the event of the week was "Sunday at Lundy's." Green draperies and maroon-colored Venetian blinds lent a bit of "luxe" to the noisy circus atmosphere where brusque waiters slithered in, out, and around tables, balancing trays laden with bluefish or a Brooklyn-brewed beer called Trommer's White Label. One Brooklynite recalls, "We went to Lundy's every Sunday, right after mass. It was very much a middle-American scene, mostly a lot of Irish and Germans, wearing huge bib napkins. The lobsters were awash in butter that dribbled down your chin, but nobody cared. The fish was done to a turn. The steamers were sandless. After Sunday dinner, you'd walk with your parents along Sheepshead Bay, inhaling the salt air and staring dreamily at the fishing boats. Sunday at Lundy's was part of growing up in Brooklyn."

Irving Lundy, the founder-owner, began his restaurateuring as a youngster, selling clams from a pushcart in Sheepshead Bay. When he died at the age of 82 in 1977, Lundy, who had never married, was a recluse who had lived for many years in an apartment above the restaurant, surrounded by sixteen Irish setters. He kept to himself because of robberies at Lundy's and the murder of a sister and a brother-in-law at their Forest Hills home. Lundy, who had acquired vast realty properties in Brooklyn and in upstate New York, left an estate valued at more than $25 million.

He also left memories of the "shore dinner" which, in the last years of Lundy's, only cost eight dollars.

Dining at the Odessa Restaurant in Brighton Beach. *Photograph © David Lee*

ginger, the Café "holds its own among the gastronomic titans of Manhattan," says *New York Times* food critic Bryan Miller. Competing with the food is the spellbinding cityscape of lower Manhattan, visible from the flower-bedecked dining room. The owner, Michael O'Keefe, says, "I believe more marriage proposals are made here than any place in the world. Teary young women line up at the telephone—calling to tell mother the news."

After traveling in Europe some years ago, and seeing how the waterfront was used in Paris, Florence, Venice, and along the Mediterranean coast, O'Keefe was stirred to create his own enchanted environment where diners could pass civilized hours, appreciating each other and the spectacle of an unreal metropolis across the river—particularly at dusk when the skyscrapers seem touched with gold. If all tables are reserved, the same sight can be seen from the bar. The River Café has its own launch and has fished people out of the East River. "If you have a window table, who knows? You might see someone jump from the Bridge in the middle of dessert—and try our banana-and-chocolate parfait," says O'Keefe, who then adds: "You know, when people jump, they too like to face the view."

Ebbets Field, home of the Brooklyn Dodgers. *National Baseball Library, Cooperstown, New York*

DEM BUMS

Zack Wheat. Nap Rucker. Babe Herman. Frenchy Bordagaray. Dazzy Vance.

What's in a name? Plenty, if you played for the Brooklyn Dodgers. Some of the names made no sense at all. Blundering, irascible, lovable, hilarious—Dodger fans would simply scream, "Ya bums, ya" with ferocity and affection throughout the team's buoyant life in Brooklyn. The Dodgers could never be charged with blandness. Even during the gloomiest hours, their oddball star names and playing power drove fans crazy. The baseball cross-talk of Abbott and Costello, a comedy duo popular during the 1940s—intense, foolhardy, blubbery—captures the "anything can happen" whacko personality of "Dem Bums," and their equally wacko adoring fans:

> You know, these days they give ballplayers
> very peculiar names. Take the Dodgers—
> Who's on first, What's on second, I Don't
> Know is on third...
> —Who's playing first?

190

Yes.

—I mean, the fellow's name on first base.

Who.

—The fellow playing first base.

Who. That's the man's name.

—That's who's name?

Yeah.

—All I'm trying to find out is, *what's* the guy's name on first base?

Oh no, What is on second.

—I'm not asking you who's on second.

Who's on first!

The Brooklyn Dodgers after their 1952 National League pennant win. *The Brooklyn Public Library, Brooklyn Collection*

If it sounds like an improbable misunderstanding, not so. According to Dodgers lore, a cabbie once stopped outside Ebbets Field while a game was underway. Calling up to a fan in the bleachers, he roared, "How're they doin'?"

"They've got three men on base!" came the breathless reply.

"Which base?" spluttered the cabbie.

191

The "Three men on a base" exchange began making the rounds in 1926 after Babe Herman hit his famous drive off the right field fence with the bases loaded and made it to third only to find that two of his mates were also there.

Inducted into the Dodgers Hall of Fame some years ago, Babe Herman said, "Everybody blamed me. It wasn't until twenty years later that Dazzy Vance admitted *he* had screwed it up. He had been on second and should have scored easy. Chick Fewster was on first and he expected Vance to score and I expected 'em both to score. I'll always be known as the guy who tripled into a triple play. Which was impossible. There was already one out."

Got it? Let's try again, then.

Who's on first?

Brooklyn, with its green fields and pastoral plots, helped popularize the sport of baseball, which had evolved gradually in the mid-nineteenth century. The borough had seventy rival teams. There were ballparks in Williamsburg, Bedford–Stuyvesant, Bushwick, and the Red Hook section where the Dodgers made an impressive debut. In their first season of 1890, they won the National League pennant. Known at one time or another as the Bridegrooms, the Superbas, and the Robins, the team's identity with Brooklyn was scored instantly when it was tabbed the Trolley Dodgers—and for a good reason. Brooklynites had to scurry across boulevards and avenues to avoid getting hit by the clanging streetcars on intersecting tracks. Later, as a team name, the Brooklyn Dodgers grasped the public's imagination. It said something about the borough and its indestructible residents. It had a melodious ring and sounded as natural as Mom's Apple Pie or plain ol' pumpernickel.

In 1912, Charles Ebbets, who started with the Dodgers as an office boy and worked his way up to club president and then sole owner, realized a dream. He built a 35,000 seat ballpark on a swampy wedge of Flatbush land—between Bedford Avenue and Sullivan Place—called Pig Town because it was a smelly dump where farmers still brought their pigs to picnic and fatten up. For sixty-eight seasons the Dodgers epitomized the heart and soul of Brooklyn, and, as a catchword, indeed, as an *institution*, became familiar to millions throughout the world. When play-by-play radio broadcasts began in the 1930s, you could follow a game by simply walking down the streets of Brooklyn and hearing who was on first, second, or third from radios perched near the windows of tenements, bungalows, stores, and cars. For decades when the Dodgers hovered near the bottom of the league, the love affair between the fans and the team never stopped. The nickname "Bums" was a term of endearment. So was the phrase, "Wait till next year..."

Brooklyn Dodgers pitcher Johnny Podres grabbed by catcher Roy Campanella after the final out of the seventh and deciding game of the 1955 World Series at Yankee Stadium, New York, October 4. Dodgers third baseman Don Hoak is seen running up to the mound. *AP/Wide World Photos*

Legends grew up around both the fans and the team. Dodger buffs recall that in the 1930s outfielder Frenchy Bordagaray tried to make it to the plate without sliding, and was tagged out. Casey Stengel, the colorful manager of the period, demanded, "Why the hell didn't you slide?" Bordagaray said he wanted to but was "afraid I'd crush my cigars." In the 1950s, pitcher Carl Erskine recalls hearing a fan in the bleachers ask, "Who's pitchin' today?" The reply: "Oiskine." The fan fretted. "What are dey tryin' to do, t'row de game?" Clem Labine observes, "Ebbets Field was small. The fans were very close to the players. Without binoculars, they could see you and you could see them. We could even *hear* 'em." Besides the catcalls, the cheers, the obscenities shouted at visiting teams, there was also music. A Brooklyn woman named Hilda Chester positioned herself in the left field bleachers holding cowbells which she jangled encouragingly. And a brass percussion ensemble of amateur musicians, calling themselves the Dodger Sym-Phony, blared joyously when an opponent struck out. Once, on Ladies Day, two guys dolled up like women were arrested for trying to get in free. Another time, about five hundred fans, unable to get seats in the sold-out bleachers, hauled down a telephone pole and used it to ram open the center-field gates.

After years of being the underdog team, the Dodgers, under Leo Durocher, won the pennant in 1941. It was the first time in 21 years.

The Dodgers' "Sym-phony" Band.
AP/Wide World Photos

Schools closed in Brooklyn. Two million people showed up to wave and shout as the team paraded down Flatbush Avenue. From 1947 to 1956, the Dodgers won six of the National League's nine pennants. Bursting with an all-star lineup that included Jackie Robinson, Roy Campanella, Pee Wee Reese, Duke Snider, Carl Furillo, and Johnny Padres, the team was magically transformed into the best team in baseball. The soaring climax came in 1955 with a World Series victory over the Yankees. Headline writers turned editorial cartwheels! DODGERS DOOD IT, BUMS AIN'T BUMS—ANYMORE! Sixty-five years after becoming a major league team, the Dodgers finally brought home their first championship.

Then, quick as a flash, the glory was gone.

It was all over for the Brooklyn Dodgers.

The team's owners were alarmed that by the late 50s, baseball viewers were fleeing to the suburbs. Brownstones in Bed–Stuy and Brownsville were emptied, boarded up, and, as minority families moved in, blocks of Brooklyn took on the sorrowful and sinister aspect of an urban wasteland. The flight was followed by a panic:

The Brooklyn Dodgers' 1941 Flatbush Avenue victory parade

neighborhoods spiralled into decline. Brooklynites wanted the Dodgers to stay put even as they themselves were leaving. The final game was played on September 24, 1957, and then the newly named Los Angeles Dodgers (the *whaaaat?*) opened a year later in southern California. Ebbets Field was demolished and replaced by a housing project. "What's Niagara without the Falls? What's Hershey without chocolate?" snorted one angry state senator. "What's Brooklyn without the Dodgers?"

The team's owners claimed it was impossible to negotiate a new and larger stadium with the city, that "Dem Bums" were squeezed out by politicos and the stubbornness of Parks Commissioner Robert Moses. Still, the transfer to California meant a tidy financial coup for the team's owners, a group headed by Walter O'Malley, who was accused of putting business before the borough's welfare. So the Dodgers of Los Angeles play on, but the mystique vanished along with the passion, and Brooklyn, which suffered a severe identity crisis, has never fully recovered from the loss.

The Brooklyn Dodgers provided baseball with plenty of fun in the form of base-path pileups and fielding blunders that often pulled the team closer to the bosom of Brooklynites than a home run. But the Dodgers also played a significant role in sports history. The Brooklyn Dodgers became America's first racially integrated team, when manager Branch Rickey put a black infielder named Jackie Robinson into play in 1947. The team, wrote journalist Roger Kahn, became "targets" for intolerance. To many players and officials the sport was a *shrine* of white supremacy. "The Robinson presence was a defilement and the whites who consented to play at his side were whores. Opposing pitchers forever threw fastballs at Dodger heads...opposing bench jockeys forever shouted 'monkey-fucker.' But the Dodgers who were at the core of the team stood together in purpose. No one prattled about team spirit. No one made speeches on the Rights of Man. No one sang, 'Let My People Go.' Without pretense or visible fear these men marched unevenly against the sin of bigotry. That spirit leaped from the field into the surrounding two-tiered grandstand." Soon Roy Campanella followed Robinson to the team. "Brooklyn made us feel at home, Brooklyn accepted us tremendously," he says.

The poet Marianne Moore summed up the spirit of the Brooklyn Dodgers when she reflected:

> "I said to myself"—pitcher for all innings—
> "as I walked back to the mound I said, 'Everything's
> getting better and better.'" (Zest: they've zest.
> "Hope springs eternal in the Brooklyn breast'..."

Jackie Robinson in 1947. *AP/Wide World Photos*

THE REEL WORLD OF BROOKLYN

In the movies, anything can happen in Brooklyn because, in fact, everything does. Throughout the years, Hollywood presented Brooklyn as a borough for Everyman—an urban locale of brutality and poverty, stability and boisterous mayhem, where pristine vulgarity marches alongside awesome sophistication. Brooklynites in *reel* life emulate the real: they come in all shapes, sizes, colors, and they astonish the ear with a variety of accents.

Hollywood portrayed Brooklyn as the source of energy and ingenuity and the slam-bang rush of American life. Sanitized "Andy Hardy" towns were put on film, but they were too limited, too restricted, too *idealized* for mainstream audiences. Gorgeous chorus girls, obscure salesmen, grizzled mobsters, European refugees, and fugitives may have done time in Peoria or Pasadena, but the Brooklyn "setting" came to represent a mode of urban universality to millions.

Where else would you find—and accept—two maidenly aunts who baked heavenly biscuits, stirred soups for sickly friends, and then gently coaxed homeless old men to drink wine laced with arsenic? Brooklyn, of course. The looney plot might happen in Allentown, but it's a lot more crackpot and believable in Brooklyn, where theatrical folklore is truth.

Thanks to Hollywood, everybody knows Brooklyn.

Spike Lee in *Do the Right Thing. Photograph Universal Studios*

Clockwise from top left: Lloyd Nolan, Joan Blondell, Dorothy McGuire, James Dunn, and Peggy Ann Garner outside their Brooklyn tenement home in Elia Kazan's *A Tree Grows in Brooklyn;* Al Pacino in Sidney Lumet's *Dog Day Afternoon;* Karen Lynn Gorney and John Travolta in John Badham's *Saturday Night Fever;* Frederic March in Laslo Benedek's *Death of a Salesman;* Cary Grant and Priscilla Lane in Frank Capra's *Arsenic and Old Lace.* *Photograph top left courtesy Universal Studios, all others courtesy Cinemafile, Inc.*

High Society

THE HEIGHTS OF SOCIETY

Brooklyn and Society?

Sounds like a contradiction. The borough, with its workaday image, and Society, with its patrician profile, don't seem to have much in common. But over the centuries the upper classes have discreetly remained in Brooklyn, and the borough, always accommodating, has taken them in stride. Even today a social scene flourishes in Brooklyn Heights, although—to be sure—nearly all of the Old Guard descendants have gone, and those who are left insist that nowadays there's no such animal as "society."

Yet in the Heights there's a core of genteel traditions that continues. "If you're going to find society in Brooklyn—whatever it *is*—you'll find it here," says Otis Pratt Pearsall, a lawyer who comes from the Pratt family that helped found the city of Hartford in the 1600s. With his wife, Nancy, and John R. H. Blum, an heir to the Abraham & Straus department store fortune, he successfully led a battle in the 1950s to arrest the Heights's long decline. Its establishment as New York City's first landmarked historic district in 1965 helped renew its attracton for families of substance.

Clubby, do-gooding, and unpretentious, the Heights's upper classes behave more like those of a small, laid-back city than their counterparts in show-off Manhattan. As with their New England forebears who flocked to the Heights in the nineteenth century, tradition still has an important role in their lives. They are likely to send their children to Poly Prep Country Day School (known as Poly) or Packer Collegiate Institute—from which, of course, they themselves have graduated—spend weekends and summers on Long Island's North shore, and belong to such organizations as the Rembrandt Club (male), the Mrs. Field's Club (female), and the Heights Casino (for tennis and squash). They also lend their energies to charities and nonprofit endeavors. And when they die, they join their ancestors in the grandest club of all, Green-Wood Cemetery. They love being from Brooklyn, where their lineage sometimes goes back for generations, and they are zealous preservers of the Heights's charming precincts.

Entrance to Packer Collegiate Institute.
Packer Collegiate Institute, Brooklyn

Otis Pratt Pearsall and his wife, Nancy, and Daughter Melissa, with poodle Jolie. *Photograph © David Lee*

Malcolm Mackay and his wife, Cynthia.
Photograph © David Lee

Previous page
Class Day, 1930, at Packer Collegiate
Institute. Packer seniors are fashionably
gowned as they carry the traditional
"daisy chain" in the Packer garden.
Packer Collegiate Institute, Brooklyn

"No one ever claimed Brooklyn, and perhaps more particularly the Heights, was on the cutting edge of change," says Malcolm Mackay, a thirteenth-generation Brooklynite of Dutch, English, and German descent. "Queen Victoria would feel right at home. Some of us won't live anywhere else." Mackay is a returnee to the borough that's the birthplace of his parents, John French Mackay, an advertising executive of long Brooklyn heritage, and Helen Pflug Mackay, whose Brooklyn ancestry goes back to the prosperous German community that settled in Brooklyn in the 1830s. Mackay, his wife Cynthia, an ophthalmologist, and their two children occupy a Greek Revival house on Columbia Heights, the bluff overlooking New York Bay edged by the Esplanade.

A walking encyclopedia of Brooklyn history, Mackay—a lawyer and, like his father, a Princeton alumnus—actually grew up in Oyster Bay where his parents had moved. But after his own marriage, he reverted to his Brooklyn roots. "It's cheaper to live and bring up kids here," he says. In his spare time, he writes articles about the borough's past and present, and serves on the boards of several of its institutions, among them the Brooklyn Botanic Garden and Green-Wood Cemetery. The Mackay children, Rob and Hope, are among the Casino's champion squash players.

ONION SANDWICHES AND SQUASH

In fact, the Mackays, the Pearsalls, and their friends are apt to meet often at the Casino, a convivial place that—apart from its use as a sports facility—is also the scene of social events, lectures, movies, yoga classes, family meals, and festivities. Built in 1904 by a group of Heights gentlemen who wanted "a country club in the city," its handsome and commodious building on Montague Street was probably the first in the country specifically designed for tennis indoors. Among its squash and tennis champions have been John J. McCloy, the banker who served as U.S. High Commissioner for Germany after World War II; William McChesney Martin, long-time chairman of the New York Stock Exchange and then the Federal Reserve Bank; and the financier Dean Mathey, for whom a college is named at Princeton.

Unlike many other Brooklyn clubs, the Casino survived hard times in the Depression, due in large part to the leadership of Seth S. Faison, a now-retired insurance executive, who came up with a plan for increasing membership. Today, with a roster of nearly six hundred, it serves as a kind of year-round family camp, and it's noted in the sports world for the number of squash champions it turns out, ranking Brooklyn—at least in this arena—as a power equal to England and Pakistan.

In contrast with the solidly planted Casino, two other veteran Heights clubs have no fixed locations at all. Viewed affectionately by their members as "anachronisms," they divide males from females—except on special occasions—and neither sex seems to mind. One is the Rembrandt Club, founded in 1880 by a dozen male worthies as the "Social Arts Club of Brooklyn" (early on, it changed its name to the Rembrandt Club, but the "social" in the original title still very much applies). The other is Mrs. Field's Club, established in the early 1880's by Mrs. Mary J. Field, a Brooklyn matron turned Manhattanite, who had lectured for some years on literary topics to a class of women "more or less prominent in society." The class eventually became Mrs. Field's Literary Club.

Rembrandt, with a membership limited to one hundred men, who still meet five times a year in black tie, is dedicated to "the promotion and encouragement of the Arts." In its younger days, the club held loan exhibitions, sponsored drawing classes in the public schools, and invited prominent artists to give lectures at its meetings. Although discussions about a permanent home for the club went on for fifty years after its founding, to this day it has no fixed meeting place. The members congregate instead at each other's houses, and gatherings have an incorrigibly traditional format. Minutes of the previous meeting are read, and then a guest speaker, male or female, holds forth. Topics range from art to music to travel to poetry to Roman Imperial coins to whaling to local architecture—but tend to avoid politics and religion. And there is always a lavish "collation," laced with champagne.

"For me, it's been a wonderfully pleasant way to meet people involved with the arts," says Seth Faison, who still misses Rembrandt's once-ample supply of Cuban cigars, cut off when Castro took over the country. The club abhors publicity, the badly-behaved, and hard liquor. "Rembrandt is elegant," Robert T. H. Davidson, a former club president, once explained. "Our speakers address themselves to elegant subjects, our traditions are elegant, and our older members who nod in the back of the room at meetings have acquired the ultimate elegance of snoozing without snoring."

The Mrs. Field's Club, likewise limited to one hundred members, is the women's answer to Rembrandt. Set up as a club in 1884, its requirement for admission was social standing rather than literary accomplishment. Still, it pioneered in nailing well-known literati—including the poet William Butler Yeats—as speakers before they had appeared elsewhere in America. "Early Fieldians were well-dressed, wealthy, handsome, with charming manners, accustomed to command and to be obeyed," wrote Sheila Holderness, a

The tennis courts at the Brooklyn Heights Casino. *Photograph © David Lee*

The Lounge in the Brooklyn Heights Casino. *Photograph © David Lee*

The original entrance to The Brooklyn Club on Remsen Street near Clinton, built ca. 1858. *Photograph Robert M. Klein. The New York Times*

former secretary of the club, on the occasion of its centennial in 1984. "They were lionesses in the streets of Brooklyn, but tabby-like in the hands of Mrs. Field."

Like Rembrandt, Mrs. Field's Club lacks a permanent setting for its luncheon meetings, and members are today more apt to congregate in public facilities than in each other's homes. Theatrical performances, songs, monologues, and occasionally even literary talks are part of the agenda, as are the traditional tiny onion sandwiches.

"There's a nice camaraderie," is how Audrey Madden, a former president of the club, describes the Field's appeal. With her late husband, John, and their children she lived for nearly thirty years in a grand, six-story brownstone on Columbia Heights, and made it the setting for both Field's and Rembrandt gatherings. "Women of all ages belong, from the thirties to the nineties. Some might view it as a frivolity that we meet and entertain each other four or five times a year, but to members it's a necessity. It provides a lovely, friendly, affectionate bond."

Another still-viable social institution born in the nineteenth century is the Brooklyn Club, established at the close of the Civil War as a refuge from home by a coterie of powerful Heightsmen. Like the Heights Casino, the club has its own building, a memento-filled mansion on Remsen Street. Today, it's mainly a lunch and dinner place for local business and professional men. The oldest active member is eighty-five-year-old John L. Livingston, who joined in 1936. Livingston, who grew up on Park Slope, is the last surviving member of Lott & Livingston, a law firm that landed its first client, the First Reformed Church of Flatbush, in 1654. Client and firm are still together.

CHARMED CIRCLES

Although Brooklyn has always had its privileged class, beginning with the early Dutch landholders and the prosperous English merchants, what might be called a social scene began to develop in the mid-nineteenth century. Already by 1840, Fulton Street was divided into "plebeian" and "aristocratic" sides. No one of wealth or prominence would dream of walking on the east, or "sixpenny," side, much less live there. And by the early 1860s, a Brooklyn upper caste had begun to define itself. Clinton Hill, the Bedford section, Park Slope, South Brooklyn, and other neighborhoods all had their social sets, but the Heights was the most fashionable dwelling place. Its attraction was enhanced by an early real estate developer, Hezekiah Pierpont (whose son, Henry, restored the name to its fancier original, Pierrepont).

A restored apartment at 139 South Oxford Street, Fort Greene. *Photograph © Phoebe Ferguson*

Like many Heights dwellers, Pierpont had New England roots—his grandfather had been the original minister to the New Haven colony—and the fabled New England practicality. A far-sighted entrepreneur, he was the country's first gin distiller, an exporter, and the backer of Robert Fulton's first steam ferry between Manhattan and Brooklyn in 1814. His mansion on Montague Street was surrounded by parkland, and he bought up all the additional acreage he could get for development. In 1816 he began to lay out wide roads, from Clark Street south to Joralemon, decreed that all houses built on them be of brick or stone, and otherwise encouraged the growth of "a select neighborhood and circle of society."

And he succeeded. A number of well-to-do Manhattan merchants and manufacturers found the Heights to their liking, among them Abiel A. Low, a China trade importer, whose son, Seth, became one of Brooklyn's great reformist mayors, then the first mayor of consolidated New York; Simeon B. Chittenden, a dry goods magnate turned financier, philanthropist, and congressman; and Alexander M. White, a fur merchant whose son, Alfred Tredway White, built low-rental housing for workers and endowed the Brooklyn Botanic Garden. As the younger Chittendens, Lows,

Whites, and other children of prominent Heights business and professional men grew up, they formed an active social scene that soon became known as the "charmed circle."

By the 1890s, three keys were needed to enter that circle: church, charity, and grandfather, according to the "History of Brooklyn," published by the *Brooklyn Daily Eagle* in 1893. "Among the descendants of the old-time merchant princes on the Heights, family and caste have been everything," notes the history. "It was a great matter to be a genuine old Brooklynite. Outsiders, no matter whom they might be, were regarded askance. Even now the portals of the Heights mansions open with care as to who is to be admitted."

CHURCH AND CHARITY

What differentiated social life in this staid enclave from that of Manhattan was Brooklynites' attachment to their homes and churches. In Brooklyn, entire families belonged to clubs, and churches were centers of social life and social influence. Life in Manhattan was less family oriented; clubs and churches had little connection with domestic affairs. In Brooklyn, church "sociables," held in private homes, were the first distinctive social events, along with private theatricals. Shortly thereafter, dancing set in, with the quadrille, the schottische, the polka, and the waltz. A young Yale student, William H. Cromwell, is credited with introducing the cotillion, or the german, as it was called, a brisk dance characterized by intricate "figures" and the continual changing of partners, which took the younger set by storm.

As the Civil War made northern inroads in the early 1860s, the call to raise money for the care of sick and wounded Union soldiers spurred the greatest social event Brooklyn had ever known, the Sanitary Fair. Held in 1864 in and around the Academy of Music on Montague Street, the two-week event enlisted almost everyone of social prominence in Brooklyn and raised $400,000 for the United States Sanitary Commission, a forerunner of the Red Cross. It entertained a vast public with an art and curio museum, an old-fashioned New England farmhouse kitchen in which costumed attendants handed out bowls of chowder from a huge iron pot, and a Hall of Manufactures that displayed the latest in consumer goods.

The social whirl of that era was lovingly described by a participant, Susan M. Van Anden, a niece of Isaac Van Anden, founder of the *Brooklyn Daily Eagle*. "Those were the days of sumptuous drawing rooms with their beautiful mirrors, crystal chandeliers, heavy furniture, Moquette and Aubusson carpets in patterns woven for the room," she wrote some fifty years later, "costly ceilings decorat-

A restored apartment at 309 Adelphi Street in Fort Greene. *Photograph © Phoebe Ferguson*

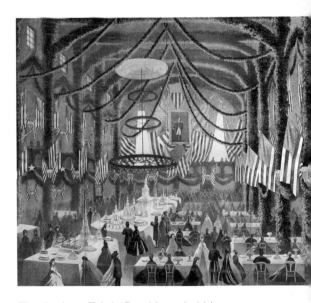

The Sanitary Fair in Brooklyn—held in support of the Sanitary Commission, which looked after the welfare of Union troops during the Civil War. *Colored engraving, 19th c.*

ed by Italian artists; the days of grand receptions, the house filled with flowers, soft music with gracious women here and there to help receive, and the dining room table gleaming with cut glass and silver, with tempting edibles in as fascinating array as a French chef could devise. Terrapin was then in vogue, with champagne freely flowing."

Formalities were strictly observed, she recalls. "No matron would think of introducing her daughter to Society other than from her own home. The invitations of those days were delivered from house to house by the hostess in her carriage, coachman and footman wearing white gloves, the latter running up and down front steps delivering the invitations with great ceremony."

Well-heeled Brooklynites also took their charities seriously, including such causes as the Homeopathic Hospital, the Brooklyn Orphan Asylum, the Brooklyn Industrial School and Home for Destitute Children, and the Children's Aid Society. One Brooklyn socialite remembered feasts that were given for the children on Thanksgiving and Christmas: "Crowds of visitors assembled on these occasions, many coming for the sole purpose of seeing how much an orphan could eat."

A mansion south of Prospect Park in Flatbush. *Photograph © David Lee*

Garden of the Sheepshead Bay Rowing Club, early 1900s. *Photograph George P. Hall. New-York Historical Society*

John Pflug, an uncle of Malcolm Mackay, at the ball after the All Star Game between the Fort Hamilton and Argentinian polo teams in 1941 at Fort Hamilton. *Malcolm Mackay*

A wide variety of clubs, most now extinct, offered other divertissements to Brooklyn blue bloods. Among them were the Hamilton, an art and literary society whose ancestry went back to Alexander Hamilton's admirers in the 1830s; the Crescent Athletic, a muscular organization focusing on football, boxing, boating, and tennis; Riding and Driving, with its vast indoor arena on Plaza Street; the Alcyone Boat Club, which held summer excursions and fall regattas; and Company A, 23rd Regiment of the New York National Guard, whose members repaired, after strenuous military drills, to equally strenuous meals and songfests.

OF HATS AND HORSES

But by the turn of the century, Heights society—as elsewhere—was at a peak of vapid consumption and display, and dress—for men and women—was at its most stilted and ostentatious. "Luxury and show were piled on," wrote Helen Appleton Read in 1933, recalling her youth as a Heights belle in the 1900s. "One had to be a great beauty to survive against the handicap of hats that sat on the top of the head without any relation to the face or the high collars and tightly boned dresses that held sway until Paul Poiret's revolutionary ideas changed the figure and clothes of the Western world."

The haute Heights, like Society everywhere, began to fade after World War I. The automobile, the spread of the suburbs, and the lure of Manhattan took many families away. "The slogan was, the nicer you were, the sooner you left," says Malcolm Mackay. Still, his mother, born Helen Pflug in 1907, the daughter of a prominent surgeon, happily recalls a privileged childhood on Stuyvesant Avenue—a once-beautiful street known as "the avenue of trees." As a schoolgirl, she attended Adelphi Academy and then the ultra-fashionable Brooklyn Heights Seminary, and was a regular at Miss Hepburn's Dancing Classes, where each girl, chaperoned by her mother, had to bring two young men. She also spent a good deal of time on horseback at the Riding and Driving Club, where her two brothers became polo champions. "You either rode or you played tennis," she says.

In the summer her family—like other Brooklyn Brahmins—took the horses, along with their grooms, to their country place on Long Island, where they performed in the horse-show circuit. During the winter season, there was lots of dancing. The season opened with the younger set's Cinderella Ball, a benefit. Tea dances, by invitation only, were held at the riding club or the Women's Club on Pierrepont Street, from 5 to 7 in the afternoon. The mandatory garb for girls was an afternoon dress and a hat. At the age of eighteen, Helen Pflug made her debut with seven or eight other young ladies at the 1925 Junior Assembly, a dance-reception held each December at the Heights Casino. And then she moved with her family to Long Island. But she remembers her years in Brooklyn as "a lovely, lovely time of my life."

The social scene in the Heights has been revived, in a very scaled-down way, by upper-caste families who returned in the 50s and 60s. But it is cozy, not grand. Most of the great old families and institutions have disappeared. And the economic and political complications of life today hardly encourage the perpetuation of an elite. Those in the Heights who still participate in social traditions wonder about their children. "Will the new generation be as willing as we were to fit into existing institutions?" asks Otis Pratt Pearsall, who points out that "new and powerful social energies" are being generated by the middle-class blacks who are coming to live in Brooklyn. "Will they get the same kick out of them that we old fogies do?"

The Poly Prep sports field at the foot of the Verrazano Bridge. *Poly Prep Country Day School, Brooklyn*

Industrial
Evolutions

During its days of glory, Brooklyn was called "America's biggest grocery and hardware store," for the sea lanes of the world ended at Brooklyn piers, making it a national commercial and industrial center. Years ago, millionaire merchants on The Heights watched their clipper ships sail off from Brooklyn to China, the Indies, and Alaska, in search of spices, tea, and fur. As the century turned, it became a major grain port, and coffee and cocoa were stored in the waterfront warehouses. It was, the novelist-critic Edmund Wilson recalled, a borough of smells—"warm fumes of chocolate from a confectionery factory." Emanating from other plants were smells of horseradish, ice cream, chewing gum, paint and varnish, ravioli and macaroni, and beer and gin.

Brooklyn's diversified output ranged from hats and harnesses, typesetting equipment and chemicals, to ships and books, porcelain and glass. There were also sugar and oil refineries and flour mills. In Manhattan, it was said, you could walk along the streets and just see building façades, but in Brooklyn all the goods of the world were laid out before you to see, smell, and touch. If you wandered down to the waterfront a spectacle of freighters flying flags of Norway, Germany, Portugal, Argentina, Brazil, and China gave Brooklyn a world presence. And before December 1941, Japanese ships docked in Brooklyn, unloading silks and glassware.

Brooklyn went through a series of seemingly limitless industrial evolutions, but after World War II, the busy hive stopped buzzing, and it would be some years before the machinery of Brooklyn began to move again.

FRONT PAGES

The *Brooklyn Daily Eagle*, a daily afternoon newspaper that began publishing in 1841 and fell silent as the borough's voice in 1955, was never as famous outside New York as the Brooklyn Dodgers, but it was as much a part of Brooklyn as the baseball team. The journalist Pete Hamill, who used to deliver it after school, observes, "It had a

Brooklyn Port Authority Pier I, looking east. *The Bettmann Archive*

The 45,000-ton battleship *Iowa* sliding down the ways into the East River. *The Brooklyn Public Library, Eagle Collection*

great function: it helped to weld together an extremely heterogeneous community. Without it, Brooklyn became a vast network of hamlets, whose boundaries were rigidly drawn but whose connections with each other were vague at best, hostile at worst."

When the presses stopped after a five-month strike—foreshadowing economic woes that would later affect other dailies in New York—Brooklynites felt an emotional shock at the loss of their venerable 114-year-old institution. *The Eagle* thrived when Brooklyn was growing and died when the borough was in decline. Until the turn of the century, it had the largest circulation of any afternoon paper in the country. In its heyday, *The Eagle* provided Brooklyn with national and foreign coverage as well as detailed local news.

Walt Whitman was editor from 1846 to 1848, when Brooklyn still used well water and stagecoaches clattered through the town. Whitman supported free trade and higher wages for dock workers, and he campaigned against slavery. Nurturing the tradition of community concern, he wrote about three thousand words a day. One editorial was headlined, "Are We Never to Have any Public Parks in Brooklyn?" Whitman revealed in *The Eagle* that the bones of hundreds of American soldiers who died in British prison ships off Wallabout Basin during the Revolution were lying in the bay. His crusade resulted in the creation of Fort Greene Park and the reburial there of the prison ship martyrs.

Personal journalism did not start in New York in the late 1960s. Walt Whitman was an old hand at it. Here in its entirety is an obituary he once wrote:

Samuel Leggett
—This man is dead. He was immensely rich. He died on the night of the 5th instant. Mr. Leggett belonged to the religious denomination of Friends, and was for a great number of years a prominent merchant in New York City. He was at one time one of the largest auctioneers, and President of the Franklin Bank just previous to its failure—by which failure, under the most abominable circumstances, he acquired a splendid property, and was at his death a large owner of real estate. Among other property, he was the proprietor of the United States Hotel, one of the largest in the city. He retired about ten years ago, from active pursuits, to his farm, where he has devoted his time to agricultural pursuits. He had some good qualities.

St. Clair McKelway, who edited *The Eagle* as the century turned, was another highly personal editor who not only wrote editorials but also shaped the policy of the entire paper into a reflection of his own personality. A crusty individualist, McKelway reportedly once said: "What's the use of running a newspaper according to the rule? The fun of having a newspaper is to run it just the way you please." But

Wallabout Market. *Postcard by the Illustrated Post Card Co., N.Y., 1905. New-York Historical Society*

Brooklyn Entrance to the New York and Brooklyn Suspension Bridge. *Engraving from a photograph by Gubelman. The Bettmann Archive*

Exterior of the *Brooklyn Daily Eagle* buildings. *Lithograph*

he nonetheless believed that journalism was a profession that must be served as loyally, intelligently, and honestly as church or state. When he began his editorship *The Eagle* had a rambunctious reputation that foreshadowed the Hecht-MacArthur play about newspaper days in Chicago, *The Front Page*. McKelway, it is said, "civilized" the staff and newsroom: he made certain there were enough typewriters to go around (some reporters scribbled stories in pencil). He also made certain every reporter had his own desk and phone. A few geezers had to polish up their spelling, too: they always seemed to stumble on the word "Joralemon," a street named after Teunis Joralemon, an aristocrat who purchased land in The Heights in 1803.

Always a crusading paper, in the late 1800s *The Eagle* came out against political bosses and for the Brooklyn Bridge. It unsuccessfully fought a movement to consolidate Brooklyn with New York City, warning, "If tied to New York, Brooklyn would be a Tammany suburb, to be kicked, looted and bossed." From 1899 to 1936, it campaigned—successfully—for a central library on Grand Army Plaza. Another successful campaign demolished the Elevated, or "The Black Spider," which rattled noisily up Fulton Street, darkening the main shopping boulevard. During the 1920s, *The Eagle*'s investigation of crime led to reform of the state's parole system. It looked into oil scandals in Washington, D.C., and ambulance-chas-

ing lawyers in New York. In its last years, *The Eagle* won the Pulitzer Prize for its campaign against organized crime and police corruption. But within the sleaze lies a dark morality tale. In the early 40s Abe "Kid Twist" Reles, a hoodlum from East New York, became the state's chief witness against the mob and sang like a canary about the rackets, mob-controlled unions, and money extorted from legitimate businesses. Guarded by policemen at the Half-Moon Hotel in Coney Island, Reles happened to "fall out of the window." A year before the *Eagle* closed, it ran a series on unscrupulous real estate block busting and lost some advertising. On one occasion, publisher Frank David Schroth wrote an angry local banker that he would never "permit an advertiser to tell me how to run the news or editorial columns of my newspaper."

The five-month strike closed the *Eagle* when its circulation was at an all-time high (137,000), when a continued rise in the paper's fortunes would only have a positive influence on the borough. But the editorial staff did not want to work for less pay than reporters in Manhattan; they did not want to feel "second-rate." Some union leaders, with Communist leanings, it was argued, were interested more in aggravating class conflicts (at a time when the white middle class was leaving Brooklyn) than in finding a way of keeping the historic daily alive—just when it was needed. A federal arbitrator concluded that the paper simply had become an "economic anachronism."

Today, Brooklyn has various small local weeklies that report community news. One of the liveliest is *The Phoenix*, which has a circulation of 20,000 and covers Brooklyn politics, business, education, and the arts. It's produced by a staff of about a half-dozen. Many articles are contributed by youngsters writing for the experience and no pay. It has received honors for legal reporting from the state bar association and for economic issues from the New York State Press Association. Its name, *The Phoenix*, symbolizes the brownstones of Brooklyn rising up again from ashes of the past.

Insignia of the *Brooklyn Daily Eagle*. *New York Historical Society*

St. Clair McKelway, editor of the *Brooklyn Daily Eagle*. *The Brooklyn Public Library, Eagle Collection*

Ships Ahoy

Most people today associate the Brooklyn Navy Yard with World War II when 70,000 workers were building ships there. But actually it goes back to 1789 when the first American Navy ship—a small frigate named *John Adams*—was built on the swampy shore of the East River. Three years later it was formally commissioned as the Navy Yard. The commandant's mansion—a model of Colonial architecture—was constructed on a nearby hill, assuring the social and official significance of the Yard, though it wasn't until the War of 1812 that the Yard's furnaces and forges began an anvil chorus for the arming of over one hundred ships.

Prior to the Civil War, the *Monitor*, a Union ironclad, was built in Greenpoint but fitted out and commissioned at the Yard. It later battled with the Confederacy's *Merrimac* off the coast of Virginia. Throughout the Civil War the Yard was open day and night as other ships were fitted out for sea or blockade duty.

Out of the Yard came the battleship *Maine*, blown up in Havana Harbor in 1898—an explosion that contributed to the Spanish-

The battleship *Missouri* passing under the Brooklyn Bridge to the Brooklyn Navy Yard for overhaul, 1945. *The Brooklyn Public Library, Eagle Collection*

American War. After the *Maine*, ships at the Yard became longer and heavier. The battleship *Arizona*, weighing 31,400 tons, emerged from the Yard just six months before World War I. It was sunk on December 7, 1941, when the Japanese attacked Pearl Harbor.

During the 30s, a heavy cruiser, three light cruisers, two destroyers, two Coast Guard cutters, and a gunboat were built at the Yard, now a fortress of brick walls with massive gateways that led to foundries, warehouses, machine shops, a power plant, and a radio station. Working around the clock, Yard employees—between the beginning and end of World War II—repaired more than five thousand ships, converted about two hundred-fifty others, and built three battleships and four aircraft carriers. Among the battleships built at the Yard, by men and women who toiled ceaselessly, was the *Missouri*, which Margaret Truman, daughter of the then-Vice President christened—and on whose decks the Japanese signed surrender documents on September 2, 1945.

After the war, aircraft carriers were the Yard's major industry. At the Yard, an experimental flight deck was installed on one carrier,

The *Oregon* and one of the great dry docks, Brooklyn Navy Yard, 1898. *Stereograph by Strohmeyer & Wyman. Photograph Underwood & Underwood. New-York Historical Society*

223

The Commandant's House at the
Brooklyn Navy Yard, attributed to
Charles Bulfinch and John McComb,
Jr., 1806. *Photograph © Andrew Garn*

225

the *Antietam*, that influenced future carrier designs. Then, in the early 50s, several carriers such as the *Wasp* and *Bennington*, arrived for conversion to jet operations. But for the new era of atomic submarines, the Yard was not an economic place to build ships, and it was closed in 1966. The piers and dry docks stood empty and grass grew wild between the ties of the railroad tracks.

Today America's former maritime center employs about three thousand people in a small industrial complex of manufacturing and warehousing for small businesses, which use only a small part of the vast arena's piers and dry docks. The saloons and dens of iniquity on Sand Street, once known as the "Barbary Coast" for sailors, now looks residential, or tries to. The swagger of sailors and their girls has moved elsewhere.

Recalling life at the Yard in the 50s, when the number of workers had dropped to about 40,000, Pete Hamill recalls, "It was still the largest single employer in the borough. I had one great job, with a thin, coughing black man who was a welder-burner and who stopped working every half-hour to drink milk. He said it coated his lungs against the filings of burnt metal. He coughed a lot anyway. We were working on an aircraft carrier named the *Wasp*, which was

Pete Hamill. *Photograph © Jody Caravaglia.* New York Magazine

Marvin E. Eisenstadt, president of Cumberland Packing Corporation, manufacturers of Sweet 'n Low, in his Brooklyn plant. *Photograph © Roy Round*

Tennyson, Anyone?

When the noon whistle blew for lunch at the Navy Yard during World War II, the Cumberland Cafeteria across the street was crammed with hungry laborers wolfing down hearty portions of meat loaf, potato dumplings, macaroni and cheese, stuffed cabbage, and Jello salads. In that remarkable era, Ben Eisenstadt, who owned the eatery, made a decent living for his family. Then the war ended. So did the long line of factory workers. He had to think of something *else* to do, quickly!

As a kid he'd assisted an uncle who made tea packets. Why not, he thought, make individual sugar packets? Hotels and restaurants thought this was a swell idea. In 1947 his new business was under way. Some years later, when his son Marvin joined the enterprise, both men were aware of subtle shifts in public taste. Consumers wanted to cut down on sugar for weight or health reasons. Why not offer a pinch of encouragement? They came up with another winner—a low-calorie sugar substitute (with saccharin) in a packet. What should it be called? Something catchy, of course. They remembered an old song grandma used to hum, set to the words of the nineteenth-century poet Alfred Lord Tennyson:

Sweet and low, sweet and low,
Wind of the western sea,
Low, low breathe and blow,
Wind of the western sea!

The Sweet 'N Low packet hit restaurants in 1958 and proved so popular that it was soon on private dining tables. "We chose a logo with a musical design," explains Marvin E. Eisenstadt, president of Cumberland Packing, "and pink as the packet color. Visible, but not distracting to the eye." The family company, which employs around four hundred, remains based at 2 Cumberland Street. It has an office in England and distribution agreements with a dozen foreign countries. "Thirty million people use Sweet 'N Low every day," says Marvin. Made in Brooklyn, U.S.A.

being refitted to accommodate jet aircraft. My job was to pile into the bulkheads with a huge 20-pound hammer and knock them flat. It was an orgy of sheer animal fury, beating and smashing those bulkheads until they fell, while the thin black man coughed and laughed. 'You some crazy white boy,' he would say.''

Like the *Brooklyn Daily Eagle*, the Navy Yard, even in its decline, continues as a symbol of loss. "Brooklyn without the Yard was not Brooklyn," says Hamill. "It's as simple as that."

MORE BEER

Besides the closing of the Navy Yard, another great industry went kaput in the "borough of the breweries" when high costs, taxes, and antiquated facilities caused the beer bubble to burst. In the early 70s, the brewers also wanted to get away from their crumbling neighborhoods. Schlitz signaled the end of a Brooklyn tradition, moving in 1973 to a streamlined plant in Winston-Salem. In North Carolina the new brewery filled 1,200 cans of beer a minute. Manufacturing was so efficient that the beer could be shipped north at a lower total expense than the cost of making it in Brooklyn. By the mid-70s, Piel's, Rheingold, and then Schaefer ("the one beer to have when you're having more than one") were memories of famous "made in Brooklyn" beers. A Schaefer executive said the unions were a problem. "It's a process industry—a chemical business. We couldn't afford to have a guy to turn the valves, another to

"Beer! Beer! Beer!" Parade of beer trucks of the Michel Brewery of Brooklyn moving through Fourth Avenue, 1933, as Prohibition ended. *UPI/Bettmann*

sip the product. It all has to be electronically controlled." So, a 345-year tradition came to an end.

The Dutch settlers of Brooklyn were exuberant beer drinkers, and the arriving British had a thirst for stout and ale. But it was the Germans migrating here in the mid-1800s who brought lager with them and built the beer business. "Brewer's Row" in Bushwick had eleven breweries within a dozen blocks. Splendiferous beer gardens, recalling the noisy conviviality of Bavarian beer halls, provided family frolics—oompah bands, dancing, and mountains of sauerkraut with sausages, all washed down with steins of beer. The *Eagle* reported in 1907 that Brooklynites (including children) consumed two barrels of beer or ale a year. At the time the borough had some forty breweries—including Ruppert, Ehret, Ulmer, Meltzer, and Trommer. The potbellied John F. Trommer never drank his own stuff. He preferred German wine.

The beer gardens and many breweries were knocked out by Prohibition and then the Depression. And after World War II a long strike by brewery workers crippled other companies, such as Trommer's, which closed. That strike, historians believe, was a bad omen for Brooklyn's beer industry. Still, others brewed on with popular advertising campaigns—the most celebrated being the annual Miss Rheingold contest. "Pick your favorite from these six lovely girls," trumpeted the promotion. Rheingold itself selected the first winner in 1940—a "radio personality" known as Jinx Falkenberg. But once the contest was launched, it was a hit in taprooms and taverns and lasted until the mid-60s.

Squibb Pharmaceutical in Brooklyn.
Bristol-Meyers Squibb Co., Princeton, New Jersey

228

Will there ever be a Brooklyn-made beer again, with or without professional models to boost sales? The Brooklyn Brewing Company, which carries a "Brooklyn Lager" label and is made in Utica, New York, wants to establish its own plant in the borough. So Brooklyn may have its own local brewery once again.

PRESCRIPTION, PLEASE

Coincidentally, two major drug companies got started in Brooklyn in the mid-1800s. What is now a printing facility for Jehova's Witnesses—a twin-factory building in Brooklyn Heights that you can't miss when crossing the Bridge—was once the plant for the Squibb Pharmaceutical Company. Until 1969 when Squibb shut down and moved to New Jersey, it turned out in Brooklyn such products as toothpaste, vitamins, and antibiotics. The closing was caused by a need for modern manufacturing operations, but Edward Robinson Squibb, who spent most of his life in Brooklyn, would have been saddened by the displacement from the airy, seaside climes of The Heights, which he knew and loved.

Squibb was born in Wilmington, Delaware, in 1819, and was taught by Quaker parents the significance of personal and professional integrity. He deplored war, but believed he could help the sick as a doctor in the navy after the outbreak of the Mexican War. Later he was assigned as a medical officer to the Brooklyn Navy Yard. Appalled that many patients died because drugs were wormy or decayed, he made it his mission to build a laboratory that produced pure drugs of uniform strength. Tight-fisted legislators approved only limited funds, which completely frustrated him. Resigning from the navy, he found research capital mostly from friends in Brooklyn.

Fear of the impending Civil War stirred him to proceed faster than ever on creating drugs and anesthetics. Opium, alcohol, and nicotine, he knew, did little to numb pain during an operation. On Christmas Eve, 1858, his Brooklyn laboratory was nearly destroyed by fire, and Squibb himself was badly burned. Nonetheless, he pressed on and perfected the formula for a *reliable* ether, which lessened the suffering for armies on both sides when the war finally came.

Many years later a young assistant, seeking "brownie points," suggested that a change in a formula would save money. Squibb answered, "I am willing to change a formula when I can improve it. But please remember that the master formula of every worthy business is honor, integrity, and trustworthiness. *That* is one formula I cannot change." He wouldn't even patent his discoveries, explaining they were "for those who need them." Squibb, whose company

Jinx Falkenberg, the first Miss Rheingold, returning after a U.S.O. tour of the Pacific Theater during World War II. *UPI/Bettmann*

became known as E.R. Squibb & Sons, gave the world a safe and controllable anesthetic. His impeccable character and devotion to science set high standards for others to follow and made the Squibb name an important part of Brooklyn.

While Squibb was discovering those decaying drugs, mixed with chalk, bark, or plaster of Paris, two German immigrants—chemist Charles Pfizer and his cousin Charles Erhart—were making medicinal chemicals in the Williamsburg section where German was spoken and they felt comfortable. Carrying Pfizer's name, their business was founded in 1849 with the slogan "Pfizer Quality"—and it was quality that won them awards in the years ahead.

The first product made at the factory was a compound to kill parasitic worms. Soon they were manufacturing iodine, borax, boric acid, and refined camphor. As operations grew, with an office in lower Manhattan, they began exporting to Europe and South America. At the turn of the century tartars for food processing and citric acid (which gives zip to soft drinks) were two key products. With sales climbing, Pfizer, who lived in a brownstone mansion at 295 Washington Avenue, acquired a villa in Newport, Rhode Island. His partner had died and Pfizer prepared to retire and have his sons run the company in which employees could buy stock.

Described once as a "conservative enterprise," expanding at a modest pace, Pfizer became a major player in scientific work during World War II, when the company passed from the family into new managerial hands. The big change came with "the penicillin breakthrough." In 1928 the British bacteriologist Alexander Fleming had discovered penicillin, but it was scarce and hard to make. In the early 40s, amid the German blitz of Britain, Winston Churchill asked President Roosevelt for American know-how in mastering this miracle drug. Several chemical houses instantly went to work, but Pfizer came up with the answer because of its experience with the fermentation process (which helped develop citric acid, when no one was thinking about antibiotics). When Allied troops landed on the beaches of Normandy in 1944, they brought penicillin mass-produced in Brooklyn. This marked the entry of Pfizer into the modern pharmaceutical world.

In 1949, after five years of research, a Pfizer team discovered Terramycin, which combats about twenty-five different diseases. Today, Pfizer has some forty prescription brand names on the market, from Procardia (for angina) to Feldane (to relieve arthritic pain). Dilucan, a recent product, is used to treat fungal infections that may afflict AIDS and cancer patients.

A multinational company, Pfizer's Brooklyn plant remains in Williamsburg where 650 are employed. In fact, Brooklyn was Pfizer's

The Pfizer Pharmaceutical plant.
Pfizer, Inc.

only plant until after World War II. In the early 1970s many companies pulled out of Brooklyn, but Pfizer stayed, making a decisive commitment to the borough's economic growth and enhancing the "quality of life" with hefty financial support for its cultural centers. Pfizer is more than a plant in Brooklyn. It's a powerful presence.

DOWNTOWN

Before the post-war urban upheavals began to affect Brooklyn, with some industries dying and others packing up, along with families, for the safer sameness of suburbia, "downtown Brooklyn"—the Fulton Street area—was a prosperous jumble of business and pleasure. When Brooklynites went into Manhattan, they spoke of "going into The City," which suggested slight conflicts between security and sophistication. Months often flew by without Brooklynites venturing into The City.

Downtown Brooklyn zigzagged around a triangular maze that included Borough Hall, the State Supreme Court, the Municipal Building, Brooklyn Law School, the Hall of Records, and banks and brokerage houses. After the thundering Elevated was dismantled in 1941, you could even appreciate "downtown's" modest grandeur.

Long Islanders shopped with Brooklyn residents at the big department stores—Abraham & Straus, Frederick Loeser & Com-

Fulton Street Mall. *Photograph © David Lee*

Preceding page

The elevated railroad going west to Borough Hall along Fulton Street. *New-York Historical Society*

Fuzzy Wuzzy

The year was 1902, Theodore ("Teddy") Roosevelt was president, and a man named Morris Michtom owned a candy store in Brooklyn. His secret passion had nothing to do with chocolate kisses. He loved to make toys—animal dolls. Soon the president would change his life forever.

Here's what happened: "Teddy," or TR, was a hunter-sportsman, and the nation was fascinated by an expedition known as "The Great Bear Hunt" in Mississippi. TR had killed grizzly bears and blacktail bucks, but this hunt was different. Coming upon a baby bear he told a herd of reporters that he would not shoot it. His gesture, accompanied by a cartoon of the bear, made the newspapers and Morris Michtom went to work, sewing his first little baby bear—with buttons for eyes. He then sent his fuzzy wuzzy to the White House asking for permission to call it "Teddy Bear." The president consented with alacrity.

Forget the chocolate kisses: kids clamored for Teddy Bears of their own. Morris Michtom began to make more. Orders arrived from department stores, wanting Teddy Bears. He closed the candy store and opened the Ideal Toy Company, which became a million-dollar business.

The country went crazy over Teddy Bears. TR's daughter posed with one. Vaudevillians joked, "The President with his clothes off is Teddy BARE." The Teddy Bear became a favorite disguise at costume parties. Lovers began giving each other BEAR hugs. And millions of toddlers cuddled up at night with their Teddy Bears.

The Teddy Bear is probably the most famous stuffed animal in the world. The original can be seen at the Smithsonian Institution.

A Farewell to the Fox: Workmen starting to tear down the marquee of the Fox Theater on Flatbush Avenue. *Photograph © Burns. The New York Times*

The Walker Theater in 1985, before it was divided into a quadruplex movie house. *Photograph © Alfred J. Butler. The New York Times*

Frieda Loehmann. *Loehmann's*

Preceding page

Abraham & Straus department store.

Photograph King's Views of Brooklyn

Zip!
Frieda Loehmann Had a Great Day
Zip!
Marlene Dietrich Came For a Stay

To her two sons and daughter she was "Momma," but to thousands of customers, Frieda Loehmann was the First Lady of discount fashions. "*Loehmann's*"—a word uttered today with nostalgic reverence and awe—was a landmark resale house that brought shopgirls and socialites to Brooklyn for over forty years. Loehmann's was talked about long before there were branches in other cities because, until her death in 1962 at the age of 89, Frieda Loehmann, "the lady in black," was as well known in the garment industry as the designers themselves. Black dress, black turban, who could forget Frieda?

A shrewd but cautious buyer and bargainer, of German-Lutheran stock, Frieda Loehmann bought and sold designer clothes, minus their labels, at absurdly low prices, scouring Seventh Avenue in Manhattan for samples. A chauffeur drove her around in a black truck. Opening in 1920, Loehmann's was a small basement on Nostrand Avenue, with only racks and a table. The family, who'd moved to Brooklyn from Ohio—Mr. Loehmann was a musician and clothing merchant—lived above the store. But soon expanding racks of taffetas, chiffons, tweeds, satins, velvets, knits, and cottons forced "Momma" to find new quarters at 1476 Bedford Avenue. Still, she kept her overhead to a minimum and operated on a cash-only basis.

Loehmann's really became a smash during the 30s—the Depression years. Seventh Avenue was pleased to do business with it. As one manufacturer said: "Frieda's way out in a corner of Brooklyn. She doesn't give us competition." She'd sell $80 frocks for $6.95. Her taste and uncanny instinct for fashion was admired by the late designer Norman Norell, who observed, "Frieda could go through thousands of dresses and know and remember each one in all its detail."

Roaming the garment industry or working in Brooklyn, she wore a shapeless—indeed, anonymous—black dress. Rumors persisted that the baggy black was a creation by Norman Norell. However, boarding the *Normandie* for Europe in the 30s, she grandly went up the gangplank wearing jewels and furs. In Paris she reveled in the costumes and decor at the Folies Bergère. "It's so *different* from Brooklyn," she once mused. She toted home objets d'art that gave her store a flamboyant belle-epoch atmosphere. Marble statues, tasseled chandeliers, mammoth tapestries, mirrors, and baroque tables made Loehmann's famous. There were also fur chairs covered with leopard for Marlene Dietrich and Lauren Bacall.

Stone lions guarded the stairway landing to the second floor. On this landing husbands and beaux patiently waited, far from the swirlwind of clothes. Frieda often stood on the stairway herself—an erect, spare figure, her silver hair pulled taut from a snow-white face, except for two crimson lollipops painted on her cheeks.

Upstairs at Loehmann's was a communal fitting room, possibly the first and last of its kind—a madcap balletic scene of legs and arms stepping in and out of pricey vestments while nervous fingers pulled at zippers. Pauline Trigère, who once visited the store, recalled, "I'll never forget the open fitting rooms. It seemed as if there were always women getting out of dresses that were too small for them."

There's still a Loehmann's in the Flatbush area of Brooklyn, but it isn't the same without Frieda, who built a $3,000,000 empire. Clothes were like people to her and she was sensitive as to how they were handled. "Pick up that chartreuse silk immediately," she'd chastise a flurried patron, who quickly obeyed *Mrs. Loehmann*. Designers who knew her, from Pauline Trigère to Bill Blass, agree that she was one of a kind.

The original Loehmann's, which became the "Fashion Landmark" in Brooklyn. *The New York Times*

pany, Martin's. A cluster of movie palaces—the Fox, Albee, Paramount— played to overflowing houses, and a very young Frank Sinatra sang onstage to shrieking fans. Why go into The City at all? To see a play or musical, that's why, for the "Broadway theater" once had a magic of its own.

Then, during the 60s, after mass middle-class exits, downtown Brooklyn, as a shopping and entertainment district, almost ceased to exist. It seemed like an aging slattern who enjoyed bad company. In 1977 the Fulton Street Mall, extending over eight blocks, was created to give back the historic old dame her good name. The mall got trees, wooden benches, and brick paving. Alas, it still has fast food, discount and electronic stores, and an extravagant number of shoe and jewelry boutiques. To its credit, the atmospheric restaurant Gage & Tollner remains, as does Abraham & Strauss, which toasted its 125th Brooklyn anniversary in 1990.

Since 80,000 people pass daily through the mall, efforts are being made to attract regional and national stores. But it still lacks panache. Many of the shops have chosen to have facelifts that will give them classier high-tech façades. They want to show off better merchandise for better customers.

BOOM TOWN

With the upcoming turn of another century, the business scene in Brooklyn went through another evolution. Now, in the 90s, after the post-war years of gloomy slump (or was it merely a slumber?) the borough is beginning to experience an economic resurgence that could never have been predicted a decade earlier.

Brooklyn, the not-quite forgotten borough that had long been a "hard sell," has received public and private investments of $2.5 billion that borough officials predict will create many new jobs by the year 2000. The financial infusion will enliven existing commerce but probably drive out the remaining mom-and-pop shops that lend the borough a special essence.

Downtown Brooklyn's access to subway and bus lines and Long Island trains; its hop-skip from Wall Street; its myriad sites (some vacant) for "industrial parks," new towers, and grand Romanesque buildings ripe for office renovation have suddenly made Brooklyn a desirable location after Wall Street and midtown Manhattan—civic leaders even talk of it becoming the city's third most popular commercial sector.

Already, the skyline is changing.

One of the biggest downtown developments is a technology-commercial complex known as MetroTech that will encompass eight new buildings and three renovations. Among its tenants are Polytechnic University, the Brooklyn Union Gas Company (experimenting with the first buses and cars powered by natural gas), and the Securities Industry Automation Corporation, the computer and communications systems for the New York and American Stock Exchanges. Chase Manhattan Bank, another MetroTech principal, which had to choose between moving its computer operations to New Jersey or Brooklyn, opted for the borough after receiving some tax breaks and energy subsidies. Chase's decision demonstrated a strong belief in Brooklyn's latest industrial evolution. (Knowing that Brooklyn's high crime rate keeps it from being a citadel of safety, Chase insisted upon high-intensity lighting, police patrols, and private security guards for five thousand technical employees who work all hours.) The Chase news stirred up a lot of excitement in Brooklyn. Borough President Howard Golden mused, "We may have lost the Dodgers, but we got Chase."

Ensconced at the new Pierrepont Plaza, on the edge of The Heights, is the investment banking firm of Morgan Stanley, which transferred its computer and back-office workers from Wall Street to Brooklyn. Others in the new building include the investment house Goldman Sachs & Company and the Royal Bank of Canada. At present, Brooklyn has no hotel, but it is hoped that a Hilton with 375 rooms will further the cosmopolitan ambience downtown. Middle-income condominiums as well as shops and multiplex cinemas are slated to go up above the Long Island Railroad Terminal at Atlantic and Flatbush avenues.

In the Sunset Park area, the Brooklyn Army Terminal, once a military supply center, and the Bush Terminal, a conglomeration of

Polytechnic University's Dibner Library, Center for Advanced Technology Building in MetroTech. *Polytechnic University*

piers and warehouses, are being renovated for small companies—printing, jewelry, sportswear, belt, and handbag manufacturers—squeezed out of Manhattan by soaring rents. To waterfront warehouses with stark views of Manhattan and the connecting bridges now come freighters from the Ivory Coast and South America laden with cocoa. Once again, Brooklyn is going global.

And the diversity of products continues. A thriving Brooklyn export company, for example, is Mona Lisa Fine Furniture, in Williamsburg, which replicates French provincial and early American "antiques"—armoires, sleigh beds, tables, rolltop desks, chairs—sent to buyers in the Middle East and Canada. The furniture is also distributed throughout the Northeast. For local consumption, Breakfast Productions, in Red Hook, bakes Danish pastries, French and Swiss bread, and about twelve thousand croissants daily for New York hotels and restaurants. The wholesale bakery moved to Brooklyn after a brief stay in Long Island City because it was cheaper and more central for quick distribution. And, for the unexpected, there's the Gargoyles Studio near the Brooklyn Museum. "Victoriana is hot today," says Edward Goldsmid, co-owner of Gargoyles Studio, which makes peacock and petal mirrors, satyr bookends, winged cherubs, angel candlesticks, and peering and eating gargoyles in such materials as stone, bronze, or pewter. The studio's decorative works are sold in department stores and gift shops, but it has done commissions for the Boston Museum of Fine Arts and the Cathedral of St. John the Divine in New York. "We export to England, too—frog mirrors, boar's heads, and Victorian busts," says Goldsmid. "Today people are calling Brooklyn a 'boom town,' and maybe they're right."

The Spirit of Brooklyn

A BLOOMIN' WORLD

Brooklyn, to playwright Arthur Miller, who remembers the elevated Culver Line that ran to Coney Island, *is the world*. "The Mohawk Indians, Arabs, Moslems...all these people, plus the Germans, Swedes, Jews, Italians, Lebanese, Irish, Hungarians and more, created the legend of Brooklyn's patriotism, and it has often seemed to me that their having been thrown together in such abrupt proximity is what gave the place such a Balkanized need to proclaim its never-achieved oneness." Brooklyn's incongruous national, ethnic, and racial mix makes it a dramatic setting for American mythology and imbues it with a particular spirit, or soul: though battered and bruised at times, it rallies with vivacity and courage.

A true Brooklynite is a rough-and-ready poker player who keeps getting lousy cards yet stays in the game. There may be beauty and goodness around, but Brooklynites are seldom surprised by the worst. They take pride in common sense, and seeing things as they are and as they might be. Most significantly, Brooklynites have an ability to laugh at bunkum and their own misfortune. In recent years the spirit of Brooklyn has been eroded by racially motivated anger and fear, but the borough's endearing sense of humor cannot be blunted. Stubbornness is another attribute of Brooklynites who represent *the world*—a stubbornness that often hides despair. Yet their souls are often shaped by an impertinent optimism and ambition and derring-do.

Richie Havens, who has toured the outside world as a singer, says, "Everywhere I go—Austria, Germany, Italy, the Scandinavian countries—I see the faces of people I know back home in Brooklyn where I was born in 1941. But the European faces have a harder mold. Brooklyn removed that hardness and gave our faces something more tender—an American quality. We talk about 'the melting pot' here. I bet the phrase started in Brooklyn."

When Richie Havens grew up in Bed–Stuy it was a multinational

Richie Havens. *Photograph © Stanley Levy. Courtesy Richie Havens*

Arthur Miller. *UPI/Bettmann*

243

Stoop-sitting is a Brooklyn sport as popular in Bedford-Stuyvesant (above) as it is in Greenpoint (below).
Photographs © David Lee

community of many accents, he observes fondly. Sure, there were brawls, but what he recalls is the harmony. "At Easter my mother cooked turkey and ham and macaroni. My grandmother made a cake that had marinated in rum for weeks. And everybody came! There was no television then, so after dinner the kids played Monopoly and shared toys. My best friend was an Irish guy named Danny Dugan, but there were also Italian pals on the block. In the 1950s, whites began moving out. I knew something was wrong; it was a time of confusion." He pauses, gazes out the window of a New York recording studio, and continues: "I feel very blessed to have been born before there were any ghettos in Brooklyn. I was raised without prejudice. *That* was the spirit in Brooklyn. When I later moved into the city, the trees and flowers were dying. But now when I return to Brooklyn where relatives live in East New York, I see that the trees and flowers are just beginning to bloom again. That's symbolic, isn't it?"

Borough president Howard Golden began his fourth term in 1990 stressing that Brooklyn youngsters from different neighborhoods must meet and learn about each other. To keep the borough's renewed spirit alive, he said, a generation must be raised free from bias—and free to walk Brooklyn streets without fear. Once, long ago, people did. The novelist Carson McCullers, for instance, has recalled browsing through junk shops in downtown Brooklyn, chatting with her druggist after supper and waving to a neighbor lady whose only companion was a little green monkey. Comparing the Brooklyn spirit that she knew to that of Manhattan, she decided that it was like comparing "a comfortable and complacent duenna to her more brilliant and neurotic sister." One of the things she loved best about Brooklyn was that "everyone is not expected to be exactly like everyone else."

McCullers appreciated the serenity of life in the borough—a serenity that today, alas, can be interrupted by a crossfire of bullets between the police and fleeing hoodlums. In the late 1980s Brooklyn—with its gangland executions, drug traffickers, and teenage wolf packs—was called by one newspaper "Murder capital of the city." The counterpoint between civility and chaos was lyrically expressed by Truman Capote. "Brooklyn is a sad brutal provincial lonesome human silent sprawling raucous lost passionate subtle bitter immature innocent perverse tender mysterious place, a place where Crane and Whitman found poems, a mythical dominion against whose shores the Coney Island sea laps a wintry lament."

NEW FACES, OLD RITUALS

Listen! The silence of a misty morning is interrupted by a church bell and then the toot of a horn on the river, and muffled noises of children . . . laughing or crying? It's impossible to tell. In East New York there were sobs and smiles when eight hundred homeless people, clasping their entire lives in plastic bags, found refuge in a new building with a courtyard with newly planted trees. The year was not 1887 when European immigrants reached out to Brooklyn for hope. It was in 1987 when the first housing for homeless families opened in Brooklyn. The venture, put together by Andrew Cuomo, the Governor's son, with government and private money, again extended hope to those who seemed to have lost their way.

And so the story of Brooklyn repeats itself with new faces and new tongues. A century ago, the poet-essayist Emma Lazarus, who lived for a while in Brownsville, produced verses expressing her faith in America. Her paean to the Statue of Liberty was placed on its pedestal in 1886—one year before her death at the age of thirty-eight.

The poet Emma Lazarus, who expressed her faith in America. *The Bettmann Archive*

> *"Give me your tired, your poor,*
> *Your huddled masses yearning to breathe free,*
> *The wretched refuse of your teeming shore;*
> *Send these, the homeless, tempest-tost to me,*
> *I lift my lamp beside the golden door!"*

Except for the Maoris, the Veddas, the Patagonians, and some lost Tasmanians, as novelist Henry Miller mused, the homeless came and still come to Brooklyn for a chance, *just another chance*, where they are lifted out of themselves by learning to dream wide awake. Realized dreams are evoked in ceremonies of new and old immigrants. The borough's half a million West Indians celebrate their freedom with a Caribbean carnival on Labor Day. Marchers costumed as sun gods, butterflies, and birds undulate along Eastern Parkway in Crown Heights. In July the Feast of the Giglio is observed in Williamsburg where many Italians, upon arrival in the nineteenth century, worked in factories. Several hundred men carry a giant spire and a boat representing freedom on their shoulders while performing a ritualized street dance.

The striking personality of Brooklyn's folklife contributes an identity missing from The Bronx, Queens, and Staten Island. Dramatist Neil Simon was born in The Bronx and raised in upper Manhattan, but his "autobiographical" plays, such as *Brighton Beach Memoirs*, are set in Brooklyn. Simon spent summers with his family in Far Rockaway, but does that mean anything to American theatergoers? He lived in Washington Heights. Does that locale have international recognition? Neil Simon perceives that in its quirky way Brooklyn is the world and the world knows Brooklyn. Theatergoers arrive at his comedies prepared with a sense of a tough-minded

Williamsburg street scene. *Photograph © David Lee*

245

West Indian Parade. *Photograph* ©
David Lee

place and for characters forever getting into trouble with their emotions and forever trying to get out of it with their wits.

SCREWBALL STYLES

With the individuality come contradictions dear to the hearts of Brooklynites. The novelist Christopher Morley recalls once asking a pleasantly drowsy woman for directions to Fulton Street. She suddenly screamed, and her face flooded with fear. She then sent him in the opposite direction while, nearby, a vendor selling bananas went on singing a madrigal. Woody Allen conjured up another street scene: a lad, saying "Good Sabbath," helps an old man across the street and is rewarded for his deed when the gent empties his pipe on the child's head. A vendor selling pretzels is chased up a tree by dogs. Unfortunately, Woody wrote, "there are more dogs at the top of the tree."

Brooklynites tend to have their idea of how the world *should* be. It's part of their charm. Douglas ("Wrong Way") Corrigan announced on July 17, 1938, that he was flying to California from Floyd Bennett Field in Brooklyn. Something went wrong. His Curtiss Robin airplane landed instead in Dublin. The flyer attributed his directional confusion to fog and rain, but his topsy-turvy tale put Corrigan and Brooklyn into flight history.

Even the director of screwball comedies, Preston Sturges, would be hard put to invent the tale of the millionaire octogenarian named John LaCorte of Brooklyn Heights who announced in 1987 a giveaway of $1,000 to young women who remained virgins until marriage. Virginity, he ruminated, was the only way to save the country. The contenders naturally would have to agree to a physical examination. Political and religious leaders were not amused. A feminist asked, "What does he want to do with virgins, sacrifice them?" As for saving the country, the New York Archdiocese of the Catholic Church said tartly, "It wouldn't be our strategy." It could only have happened in Brooklyn.

And what about the famous Egg Cream you've heard about—a confection whipped up in Brooklyn? It has neither eggs nor cream. Three tablespoons of chocolate syrup and one-third cup of cold

Douglas "Wrong Way" Corrigan.
UPI/Bettmann

The Man from Lake Wobegon Rediscovers the Brooklyn Beat

Garrison Keillor's *A Prairie Home Companion* had a long run on public radio (1974-1987) with his fireside stories about the people in the Midwest who lived near mythic Lake Wobegon in Minnesota. He took to the air again with his *American Radio Company* in the fall of 1989 and selected Brooklyn as the site of his broadcasts. Keillor's show, at the Brooklyn Academy of Music, was the first live variety program to emanate from New York since the early 50s when "the glamorous and unpredictable Tallulah Bankhead," as NBC warned listeners, hosted *The Big Show*. Keillor chose Brooklyn because of its intimate opera house—and a remembered feeling of unabashed openness that made him love the city.

Keillor first saw Brooklyn on a trip east in August 1953. He was eleven years old. To the youth from Minnesota, Brooklyn had a grandeur of its own. He was too young, he recalled, to consider the borough as an adjunct to Manhattan. He watched the Dodgers from the right field at Ebbets Field and rode the Cyclone at Coney Island, but his most vivid memory is of taking a walk on a hot night with his Dad where he saw a park full of people talking and cigarettes glowing, and on the grass, he continued, "families sleeping, each family on a blanket, the kids snuggled close to their mothers and fathers. I suppose people don't do that anymore, but it's how I think of Brooklyn anyway."

milk are poured into a tumbler. Then a half-cup of seltzer is added. The ingredients are lustily stirred until a frothy head rises to the top. Now, drink your Egg Cream.

DIGGING DEEP

Brooklyn's future is emerging from its vivid and substantial past. Sometimes it is seen most effectively in personal odysseys. Like a character from *Raiders of the Lost Ark*, one young man of independence and brio named Robert Diamond embarked on a passionate mission, solved a century-old mystery with his native Brooklyn wits (or divination), and is carrying on the borough's tradition of conquering new worlds.

The Long Island Railroad tunnel.

Photograph © David Lee

The intrepid Diamond, whose interests are archaeology and history, was nineteen years old and a student at Pratt in 1979 when he first heard about an abandoned railroad tunnel under Atlantic Avenue. Facts were few: it had been built by the Long Island Railroad in 1844 because the burgeoning avenue already had too much traffic for a train and, anyway, its incline was too steep for the steam locomotives. The tunnel was used for sixteen years as a rail link to a ferry across the river—then sealed and forgotten. The passage once roused the curiosity of *The Eagle*. If it existed, where was it? *Eagle* sleuths tried to find an entrance, but gave up. Questions remained: in the ensuing years, had it been a hideaway for slaves, smugglers, bootleggers? Stories circulated that when there was a full moon a

The intrepid Robert Diamond at the entrance to the Long Island Railroad tunnel. *Photograph © David Lee*

The Long Island Railroad tunnel under Atlantic Avenue, c. 1844, from an engraving. The tunnel was used for only sixteen years before being forced to close by an ordinance against steam locomotives.

steam whistle and the chug of a train could be heard under Atlantic Avenue.

Diamond became obsessed with the "lost tunnel." For almost a year he studied street maps, newspaper clippings, engineering drawings and blueprints in libraries, looking for clues. He learned that the tunnel ran for five blocks between Boerum Place and Columbia Street and that it was about 35 feet below Atlantic Avenue. He found that realtors who hoped the avenue would become a "showplace" boulevard made deals with politicians to have the tunnel closed—filled in and paved over. To make the closure legal, a law was passed against the operation of underground steam locomotives.

Now, how to unearth the tunnel? Diamond decided that the only way in was through a manhole on Atlantic Avenue. His first descents, with an air tank, a walkie-talkie, and a cable tied to him, were made in the early 80s with the assistance of Brooklyn Union Gas. Digging through soil with his hands as he inched forward on his stomach, he eventually found himself up against a brick wall that sealed off the entrance. But the wall had an airhole plugged up with rocks. Pulling them loose he suddenly stared down a 14-foot drop to the tunnel floor. Outside on the street, Brooklynites clapped and cheered. "Finding the tunnel was a miracle," his mother recalls, "another miracle of historic survival in Brooklyn."

Inside the tunnel, Diamond stood bedazzled. "It was like stepping out of the 20th Century and being transported back to the year 1861. I saw notches where the railroad ties had been. I found discarded horse-shoe spikes, parts of a whiskey jug and a pair of high-button shoes. The tunnel was perfectly preserved with brick walls and an arched ceiling of Roman architecture." His discovery received landmark status. Diamond, who now prints a tunnel newsletter and gives guided tours of "the world's oldest subway tunnel," established the nonprofit Brooklyn Historic Railway Association. He's raising money to turn the tunnel into a museum that will have its own trolley connecting cultural sites, from Grand Army Plaza to the Fulton Landing.

Where others failed or merely reveled in rumors of the tunnel, the self-motivated Robert Diamond succeeded—and is building a life for himself from Brooklyn's past. Radiating a freshness and vigor that symbolizes the borough, he says, " I think Brooklyn is one of the best places in the world to live. Once the revitalization is completed, *everyone* will want to be here."

Last seen with a bold smile on his face, the subterranean explorer was descending into the tunnel with an American flag.

"Welcome Back to Brooklyn" at the arch in Grand Army Plaza. *Photograph* © *Tony Velez*

WELCOME BACK TO Brooklyn
SUNDAY JUNE 10, 1990. GRAND ARMY PLAZA

BIBLIOGRAPHY

The Brooklyn Public Library and its reference service were of invaluable help. The *Brooklyn Fact and Trivia Book*, edited by Harriet Lyons and Nanette Rainone, and the *Neighborhood Book*, edited by Nanette Rainone, both published by the Fund for the Borough of Brooklyn, provided illuminating statistics. The Brooklyn Economic Development Corporation offered informative overviews of the borough's future.

Allen, Woody. *Side Effects*. New York: Random House, 1975.

Bergen, Teunis G. *Register, in Alphabetical Order, of the Early Settlers of Kings County*. Polyanthos (reprint), 1973.

Brown, Henry Collings. *Glimpses of Old New York*. New York: Privately printed for the subscribers of the Anderson Galleries Building, 1917.

Burnham, Alan, A.I.A., editor. *New York Landmarks: A Study and Index of Architecturally Notable Structures in Greater New York*. Middletown, Conn.: Wesleyan University Press, no date.

Callender, James H. *Yesterdays on Brooklyn Heights*. New York: The Dorland Press, 1927.

Chisholm, Shirley. *Unbought and Unbossed*. Boston: Houghton Mifflin, 1970.

Christopher Morley's New York. New York: Fordham University, 1988.

Edmiston, Susan, and Linda B. Cirine. *Literary New York*. Boston: 1976.

Eels, George, and Stanley Musgrove. *Mae West*. New York: William Morrow, 1982.

Everdell, William R. and Malcolm Mackay. *Rowboats to Rapid Transit: A History of Brooklyn Heights*. New York: Brooklyn Heights Association, 1973.

Goodwin, Maud Wilder, editor. *Historic New York During Two Centuries*. New York: G. P. Putnam's Sons, 1897–99.

Green, Gerald. "A Memoir." *Brooklyn Botanic Garden Newsletter* (Summer 1985).

Hamill, Pete. "Brooklyn—the Sane (Same) Alternative." *New York Magazine* (March 2, 1969)

Hazelton, Henry Isham. *The Boroughs of Brooklyn and Queens, Counties of Nassau and Suffolk*. Vol III. New York: Lewis Historical Publishing Co., 1925.

Hoogenboom, Olive. *The First Unitarian Church of Brooklyn—150 Years*. New York: The First Unitarian Church, 1987.

Horton, Philip. *Hart Crane: The Life of an American Poet*. New York: W. H. Norton, 1937.

Howard, Henry W. B., editor. The Eagle *and Brooklyn: The Record of the Progress of* The Brooklyn Daily Eagle. New York: The Brooklyn Daily Eagle, 1893.

Kahn, Roger. *The Boys of Summer*. New York: Harper & Row, 1971.

Kay, Helen. *The First Teddy Bear*. New York: Stemmer House, 1985.

Kazin, Alfred. *A Walker in the City*. New York: Harcourt, Brace, 1951.

Latimer, Margaret, editor. *Brooklyn Almanac*. New York: The Brooklyn Educational and Cultural Alliance, 1984.

Mackay, Malcolm. *The Heights Casino: The First Eighty Years*. New York: The Heights Casino, 1985.

McCullough, David W. *Brooklyn . . . And How It Got That Way*. New York: Dial Press, 1983.

McGowan, Martha. *Growing up in Brooklyn*. New York: Brooklyn Union Gas, 1983.

Mayer, Grace. *Once upon a City*. New York: Macmillan, 1958.

Miller, Henry. *Black Spring*. New York: Grove Press, 1963.

Mitchell, Broadus. *Alexander Hamilton: The Revolutionary Years*. New York: Thomas Y. Crowell, 1970.

Morris, Lloyd. *Incredible New York*. New York: Random House, 1951.

Moscow, Henry. *The Book of New York Firsts*. New York: Collier Books, 1982.

Murphy, Mary Ellen and Mark, and Ralph Foster Weld, editors. *A Treasury of Brooklyn*. New York; William Sloane Associates, 1949.

The Rembrandt Club. *Rembrandt Club History: The First Century*. Privately published for the members of the Rembrandt Club, 1980.

Rosten, Leo. *Religions of America*. New York: Simon and Schuster, 1975.

Rosten, Norman. *Neighborhood Tales*. New York: George Braziller, 1986.

Sanger, Margaret. *Margaret Sanger: An Autobiography*. New York: W. H. Norton, 1938.

Schroth, Raymond A., S.J. The Eagle *and Brooklyn: A Community Newspaper, 1841–1955*. New York: Greenwood Press, 1974.

Sills, Beverly. *Bubbles*. New York: Bobbs-Merrill, 1976.

Smith, Betty. *A Tree Grows in Brooklyn*. New York: Harper & Row, 1943.

Stebben, Gregg. "Who Killed the King of Hearts?" *Quest Magazine* (July–August 1988)

Stiles, Henry Reed. *The Civil, Political, Professional and Ecclesiastical History and Commercial and Industrial Record of the County of Kings and the City of Brooklyn, N.Y., from 1663 to 1884*. New York: W. W. Munsell, 1884.

Tarzian, Charles. "America's First Cultural Center." *The Phoenix* (Summer Supplement 1986).

Tynan, Kenneth. *Curtains*. New York: Atheneum, 1961.

Van Derzee, Charlene Claye. *An Introduction to the Black Contribution to the Development of Brooklyn*. Exhibition catalogue. New York: The New Muse Community Museum of Brooklyn, 1977.

Van Rensselaer, Mrs. Schuyler. *History of New York in the Seventeenth Century*. Vol. I. New York: Macmillan, 1909.

Weld, Ralph Foster. *Brooklyn Is America*. New York: Columbia University Press, 1950.

Weld, Ralph Foster. *Brooklyn Village: 1816–1834*. New York: Columbia University Press, 1938.

White, Norval, and Elliott Willensky, editors. *A.I.A. Guide to New York City*. New York: Macmillan, 1988.

Wolfe, Gerard R. *New York: A Guide to the Metropolis*. New York: New York University Press, 1975.

Wolff, Geoffrey. *Black Sun*. New York: Random House, 1976.

INDEX